Independence Day

Independence Day

A People's History

Veena Venugopal

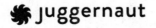

JUGGERNAUT BOOKS
C-I-128, First Floor, Sangam Vihar, Near Holi Chowk,
New Delhi 110080, India

First published by Juggernaut Books 2022

10 9 8 7 6 5 4 3 2 1

P-ISBN: 9789393986054
E-ISBN: 9789393986061

Typeset in Adobe Caslon Pro by
R. Ajith Kumar, Noida

Printed at Thomson Press India Ltd

To Kiera, with infinite hope

We are not makers of history, we are made by history.

MARTIN LUTHER KING JR.

Contents

Introduction

One Independence Day, a few years ago, a photograph of a school in remote Assam made the rounds. It showed two frail teachers and two tiny students, standing ramrod straight in chest-deep water, saluting the national flag. There had been a flood that day, but it did not stop the teachers in this school from raising the national flag, nor did it stop young Haider Ali Khan and his friend from wading through dangerous waters and reaching the school for the event.

The ferociousness of the boy's patriotism, augmented by the utter poverty of the surroundings, at first, made me tear up, and later, filled me with shame. Most of us in the country take our freedom for granted. 'This is my house,' we say easily, or 'This is my street.' And just as easily, 'This is my country.' We use these arguments when it is convenient to us, an easy means to assert our rights. Our freedom has cost us nothing and perhaps that is why we don't feel the need to wade through floodwaters to attend the hoisting of a flag. Ours is a complex and complicated country – it provides us convenient excuses. And we are beginning to forget what it took to get here.

India's freedom was a cherished victory after nearly two hundred years of struggle. Hundreds of thousands paid for this with their lives. They battled for their dignity, to be treated as equals, as fellow human beings. On 15 August 1947, there were some three hundred and fifty million Indians. Most of those three hundred and fifty million have died, but some are still alive. Who were they? What are their memories of that extraordinary moment? And how do they feel about the country they saw birthed? This is what this book is about.

This generation is now at least seventy-five years old. By the time they were born, in the late 1930s and early 1940s, the freedom struggle had taken centre stage in everyone's lives.

They were the ones trotting along beside their mothers and fathers, marching to the town hall. It was their elder siblings who were learning national songs and inspiring others to join the movement. The country was a dream, a fantasy their parents spun when they put them to sleep.

A year ago, I began this pursuit to find out what ordinary people made of the first Independence Day. Did they think they would go to sleep one night and wake up to a brand-new reality the next day? Were they part of the 'wild scenes of jubilation in Delhi' and the 'frenzied enthusiasm in Bombay'? as was reported in the newspapers the following day.[1]

Were they unquestioning devotees of the leaders of the freedom movement and did they think they would submit themselves to the cause of building a new country? I wanted to know the stories of Independence Day that the history books do not tell us.

The first step to finding these narratives was to cast a wide net. The base criterion was simple. The person had to be over seventy-five years of age. This was easy enough. But people who are seventy-five or seventy-six were too young to remember anything from that time. So I narrowed it down to those who were at least four or five years old in 1947, ideally older. Next, I wanted to make sure I covered various parts of the country.

The most evocative stories of common people from that time are usually about the Partition. But I also wanted to know what happened in Madurai on that day. And Champaran. Baroda. Palakkad. Mysore. What was the Muslim experience like? How different was it from that of the Hindus? What about the Dalits? How did their story pan out?

Most people I spoke to were children at the time of independence. A few were young adults. But even so, the rhetoric of the movement was so pervasive that they all knew about it. In Lahore, Sarabjit Singh could sense the disquiet of impending Partition based on the anxiety in the adults' conversations he overheard.

Ambika Menon, in Kerala, was privy to a wide range of debates and discussions about the freedom movement as her uncles, mother and grandmother discussed the headlines each day. The newspaper was distributed upon arrival, with each person getting a page before swapping them around.

In much of North India, pre-Partition riots stained the euphoria of the prospect of independence. But Girija Viraraghavan did not hear about it even though she was in a big city like Bombay. The further you went from Punjab and Bengal, the milder was the impact of communal tension. Perhaps the age of these storytellers, too, is relevant. In Champaran, Narendra Bhagat reasons his parents did not talk to him about the killings and massacres because they felt he and his siblings were too young to be exposed to it.

Parts of South India were particularly insulated from the churn of the freedom movement. S. Vedapuri, who grew up in the North Arcot district, and later went to Madras for college, had never seen a white person. Britain's occupation of India was merely conceptual to him, and he could not visually corroborate its existence. In Thiruvannur, Singaravelu Venkatachalam too had trouble imagining who the British really were.

'People are trapped in history and history is trapped in them,' said James Baldwin. The idea of this book is to pry out the history that is trapped in people. We have all read accounts of the first Independence Day, watched grainy footage of Pandit Nehru and Lord Mountbatten making their way through thronging masses at Red Fort. Everyone was celebrating, we thought. This was a moment that presumably united us all. That was far from the case.

Ved Prakash Malhotra, who lived less than five kilometres away from where Nehru was speaking, had no idea the event was happening. He and his family were busy patrolling their streets and trying to keep themselves safe. In Mysore, S. Narendra and his family held a clandestine celebration on 15 August 1947. The maharaja of Mysore was yet to accede to the Union and celebrating India's independence was not allowed in the princely state.

In Krishnanagar in Bengal, Tarun Kumar Roy celebrated Independence Day twice: on 15 August 1947, they hoisted the Pakistan flag since that part of the country fell on the other side of the border, and then four days later, the district was reassigned and they held a second ceremony, this time as part of India. Sarabjit A. Singh and his parents were distraught on the day. They had lost everything in the Partition and did not see any reason to celebrate. India is a diverse country, and its responses to Independence Day, too, were equally diverse.

What is common to all the stories though are the icons of the freedom movement. Everyone knew Gandhi and Nehru. Most of my subjects admired and loved Nehru. Some made career and life decisions to help build on his vision for India. Ambika Menon even poked him to make sure he was real! Panditji's word counted for everything in Saeed Naqvi's house in Mustafabad, so much so that they were certain the country would never be partitioned.

Gandhi was, of course, the enduring icon of the freedom movement. It felt like he was a part of everyone's family, Girija Viraraghavan said. Even the news that Gandhi was visiting a town close by was thrilling enough for Venkatachalam. Some were less taken in by him. As a young boy, Ganpat Aiyar was unimpressed when he heard Gandhi speak, he found his voice too thin and lacking gravitas. Yet most of my subjects recall his death vividly, some even more so than Independence Day itself. They all remember with great clarity what they were doing at the time they heard the news.

When you stitch history together from the fabric of lived experiences, it brings to light some unknown stories and brings to life some unreal ones. Memory is the fuel and the folly of oral history. The mind does not have the ability to distinctly differentiate between events seen and those narrated. Some incidents are so significant that they can never be forgotten. Others are knitted together, post facto.

Sahib Singh Virdi can still see the sun set at the end of the day when they started walking from their home in Gorala Lallian to Amritsar. Kumud Pawde can still hear the reverberations of the Sanskrit chants of a thread ceremony that she was not even allowed to enjoy from the streets because of her caste. In Baroda, Ravindra Pandya cannot forget the sight of the man who was injured in the riots after Gandhi's murder, who bled all the way down the street and into the home of the doctor in the neighbourhood. These events are burnt into their brains.

And yet, memory can be an unreliable friend too. Ambika Menon distinctly remembers the flag being raised in Doon School on 15 August 1947. Yet, when she really thought about it, she wasn't sure whether it was the snapshot of something that had happened or something that she imagined. Several times, the date of the event and the age that the interviewees thought they were did not line up. Most people thought they were older than they were at the time, implying that they had woven a later understanding of the event to what they had actually seen.

Others like Tarun Kumar Roy remembered and recorded everything, even the name of the village drunk. Despite some inconsistencies, in speaking to these people, who are a couple of generations removed from the internet and mobile phones, it was astonishing to me how much they could recall. Maybe, there were fewer distractions. Maybe, the nation was a bigger cause to them and documenting its history, even if just for their own selves, was an important task of the citizenry. Oral history is not to be confused with recorded history; it is not a replacement to what is in the books, but a supplement to them. These are the stories of incidents remembered, not events recorded. Memory is fallible and often hope, dreams and aspirations thread through it.

As this generation grew up, the country grew older. Some of the early promises were forgotten. There was often some calamity or the other. But there were celebrations too. The country accomplished a lot. On some aspects, it moved fast; on others, it floundered. And somehow, here we are, seventy-five years later.

My own relationship with the country has been complicated. This last decade has made it even more so. The political and social polarization seems daunting now, irreversible even. I often wonder where this is going to end.

Will there be a civil war? Will we prioritize and deal with climate change? Will the neighbourhood remain safe? Will we have to go to war? What about my child? What kind of a country will she inherit? Most mornings when I scan the headlines, I feel a sense of betrayal, of defeat.

Yet, in speaking to the people featured in the book, what I mostly encountered was optimism. They had seen and sacrificed so much, faced so many disappointments and yet they were overwhelmingly optimistic. There are issues, they conceded, but we need to solve them and not be weighed down by them. We are old, most of them seemed to suggest, but the country is young. It will get there, they urge, and we will find a way. In listening to them, the full extent of my own cynicism was revealed to me. Their accounts inspired me to look around myself with a little more enthusiasm, to not be afraid to roll up my sleeves and get down to the business of making the country a better place. Be patient, they said. And passionate. Neither is easy, but if anything is worth it, I daresay, it is this country.

1

The Line on the Ground

Tarun Kumar Roy was born in 1929. He worked in the customs
department until retirement. He has one daughter and lives
in Kolkata.

I was born on 5 September 1929 in Noakhali, in today's
Bangladesh. My ancestral village was called Pachpaika in
Dhaka district (Dacca, as it was spelt then), and to reach
there one had to get off the train at Narsingdi, which was
forty-eight kilometres north of Dhaka, and then travel
nineteen kilometres by boat and then another two and a
half kilometres by foot. My ancestral home, my mother's
ancestral home, and even my in-laws' home were in the
district of Dhaka, though I was not raised there.

Till the age of nine, I lived in Dinajpur where my father
was employed in government service. His name was Sailesh
Chandra Roy and my mother's, Binapani. In 1938, we moved
to Krishnanagar, in West Bengal's Nadia district, as my

9

father got a transfer there. A few months before we left in 1938, my elder brother and I were enrolled at the Dinajpur Zilla School, and when we reached Krishnanagar we were enrolled at the Krishnanagar Collegiate School. Later, I did my Intermediate and BA degree from Krishnanagar Government College. My father did not have a lot of land. Originally, ours was a well-to-do zamindari family, but our ancestors had wasted a lot of that away. We all had to learn English and get a job to survive. My grandfather took up a government job after passing his FA examination (First Arts or FA, as it was then called, was a graduate degree). Since then, this has become our 'family profession'.

In 1942, Gandhi launched the Quit India movement. I was then about thirteen years old. Many Congress leaders were arrested. I remember the photos of Gandhi, Nehru, Sardar Patel, and others, published in the *Anandabazar Patrika*, as they were being taken underground. Every day, the papers brought news of clashes between the police, the army and the public. There were accounts of railway tracks being uprooted, about post offices, banks and railway stations being looted, and trains set on fire. The movement had gripped the entire country, but its effects were not felt in Krishnanagar.

In the first few weeks, at least, it was entirely peaceful. There was no violence or demonstrations. But we did feel the sense of an impending doom. There was a strange silence everywhere. Then there was some picketing at school gates and students were stopped from entering. I remember going to school one day and we were not allowed to enter the gates, so I went back home.

A few days later, I woke up one morning and saw that 'British Quit India' was written on walls throughout the town. We heard that the night before some railway coaches were set on fire near the station. The British had an airbase in Dubhulia, which was close by. Members of the British Royal Air Force (RAF) used to travel through the city on trucks. Earlier, we had never seen the RAF people carry weapons. But now we saw that there were far more trucks and everyone in them was fully armed, some had revolvers, others had pistols. Some even had submachine guns.

Many of these soldiers had passed through the town before and were familiar faces. When they saw us, young boys, looking at them with curiosity, they usually smiled. But that day, they seemed to be giving us a smile of challenge, as though they were saying, 'Let's see how you can take your independence from us.' There was a feeling of hostility and tension on both sides.

Soon after, processions began in the town. I joined the first procession that moved from the high street to Golapti to Malo Pada to the Judge's Court and the main hospital, and finally came to a stop in front of the college. We didn't see police anywhere, but near one of the crossings, the district magistrate – Islam Sahib – showed up. He alighted from his car and told some of us to go home. Then he drove off. We didn't listen to him. Instead, we shouted slogans with renewed vigour.

I participated in this with a great deal of excitement and enthusiasm. My mother and sisters saw me march from the balcony. My father saw me too when the procession passed by the court where he worked. Later, he took me aside and told me that he had a large family and he was a government employee, and my participation in these processions might result in him losing his job. Then it would be difficult to support the family and get my sisters married. I realized the gravity of the situation and decided that I would not take part in any of these processions again.

By 1946, we were full of hope. It had become clear by this time that independence was not far away. We hoped that the Muslim League would be defeated and that India would remain undivided. I was then almost seventeen, nearly an adult. In school and in the neighbourhood paras, we used to have heated debates about what independent India would be like. At this time we were quite confident that Muslims would ignore the demand for a separate country, and that India would gain independence as an undivided nation.

The division between the communities was, however, gaining traction through the year. The riots in my town of birth, Noakhali, began in October, right after Durga Puja. In these riots there were more cases of forced conversion and rapes than Hindus actually being murdered. In the rural areas, with their open fields, the scope of killing people was not very high and there weren't too many people to begin with. But the events that occurred made us realize how vulnerable we were.

Socialist ideals or democratic conduct were no longer our prime motives. We were simply concerned about how we could live with dignity. Times were so uncertain that even this basic premise – a life of dignity – had shrunk to a great degree. The political situation was such that if there was communal violence, the authorities would not offer protection, and if a riot were to break out, our lives and property would be in peril. Amidst this anxiety and concern, we began collecting firearms in secret and learned how to make bombs. We would go to the college gymnasium, where we worked out, built our physical strength and also learnt how to fight.

Shantipur was a town nineteen kilometres away from Krishnanagar. The police were conducting a raid there and trying to recover bombs and guns, when suddenly a hail of bullets came from inside. The police were still outside the building at this point. They returned fire and finally the people in the house surrendered. This group was well known locally. They were called the Bombard Military and almost all of them were former soldiers who had experience of fighting in the Second World War.

They were handcuffed and tied and marched nineteen kilometres – nearly a four-hour journey – and brought to the jail in Krishnanagar. The incident gave us a bit of confidence, and we began to think that if a riot was to occur, Hindus would not just give up and allow themselves to be killed.

Just a few days before this incident, in Noakhali, Muslims had surrounded the home of Rajendra Lal Roy. He was a lawyer, a former president of the Noakhali Bar and a prominent leader of the Hindu Mahasabha. He and his family spent all night keeping the rioters at bay.[1] When the attackers ran out of bullets, it was said they killed all the family members and committed suicide themselves. This incident – and the courage displayed by the Bombard Military – inspired us for an armed resistance, and we began to prepare ourselves.

A man called Arun Ganguli, who was a World War veteran and trained sniper, and a few former soldiers, began to train us. We were a motley group of boys from the neighbourhood, teenagers and young adults. During the Second World War, a black market had emerged in Calcutta for guns, revolvers, rifles and pistols. After the 1946 riots in Calcutta, this market flourished even more. The buyers and sellers were all Hindus. Across the state, Hindus amassed a vast quantity of firearms, cartridges and bullets from there. Interestingly, Muslims used knives, swords and acid bulbs in these riots. There weren't too many people among them who could use firearms. To prepare ourselves, we also developed our connections in this black market.

Around this time, the District Magistrate, one Mr Naseeruddin, summoned my father. The matter was serious. My younger brother, Shyamal, was a student of Class 10 in the collegiate school at the time. One of his classmates, a boy called Hyder Ali, used to live in the government quarters of the headmaster of the school. He was related in some way to the DM. One day, Hyder saw that Shyamal was carrying a knife tucked into the waistband of his half-pant. He immediately told the DM what he had seen, who then summoned our father. Ultimately, he did not have to go meet Naseeruddin. My father's boss – who was in the Indian Civil Service – spoke to Naseeruddin, and he dropped the matter.

Around this time, just before the Puja holidays, a quarrel broke out between two of my classmates, a Hindu and a Muslim. Usually, such squabbles died down in no time but because of the kind of suspicions and competition between the two religions at the time, the quarrel escalated.

Suddenly, we saw one of them had gripped the other's throat, and fellow Muslims had surrounded the duo and were trying to drag the Hindu boy towards their hostel. Both boys were strongly built, but the Hindu boy was slightly short, while his opponent was very tall. So, the Muslim boy had an upper hand. Once I saw what was happening, I called some of my other friends. We got sticks and mallets from the gymnasium, and we walked into the fight and managed to get our guy out.

The girls of the class were kept inside the gymnasium, and people stood guard outside. Some of the boys standing guard were carrying pistols! Then the principal heard all this commotion and came running out. It was because of his intervention that we all finally calmed down. Had the principal not been there at that time, a riot could have broken out in Krishnanagar on that day.

The riots in Calcutta continued intensely for four or five days. There were incidents of rioting that carried on, in fact, for over a year, going on until Independence Day in 1947. However, even though there were no communal riots in Krishnanagar, there was tension in the air and a lack of trust between the two communities. A spark could have set off a fire. The situation was such that we were afraid to travel and were especially terrified of desolate places.

In fact, we were scared of being alone with our own Muslim friends. These were the same people we had once been very close to. In the past, we would have snuck off together to a field across the river and eaten stolen chickpeas. We had danced with them with our sticks on Muharram; we had gone on picnics together. Suspicion had now crept into these relationships. There were some sensible people on both sides, thankfully, and the people of the town were liberal in their outlook. That is why Krishnanagar was spared the riots.

The year 1947 came, and with it arrived fresh fears. The end of British rule was imminent, but a sense of uncertainty had crept into the minds of the non-Muslims in Punjab and Bengal about the partition of India and the creation of Pakistan. However, we nursed a small hope that India would remain undivided, even though to be honest, there was very little basis for such a hope.

Most Bengali Muslims wanted the country to be partitioned. At this time though, we did not feel the sense of suspicion and strangeness about the other community that we had felt during the riots. Although we could not revive the kind of affectionate relationship we had had with our Muslim friends and classmates, it became easier to talk to them again. But in our conversations, we would consciously avoid any talk of politics, even though we were seventeen or eighteen years old, and the situation of the country was such that it was not easy for us to not discuss politics.

I remember, there were a few shops on the ground floor of our house, and there was a man named Bijit Lal Chattopadhyay who had a tailor shop there. He was called Madhaai, and he was the younger brother of Bijoy Lal Chattopadhyay who was a pro-Gandhi poet, author, littérateur and somebody we revered and respected. But Madhaai was the complete opposite of his elder brother. He used to drink too much, and people called him Madha Gunda behind his back because of his unruliness.

One day, Madhaai drank too much and picked up bricks from the road and threw them at some of the shops that lined the street. The shopkeepers were Muslim. The moment Madhaai threw the bricks, they came out and started beating him up. It became very clear that it was their pent-up rage and uncertainty that was finding release, like a pressure cooker releasing steam. What Madhaai had done cannot be condoned, but a tolerance for drinking was an old tradition in Krishnanagar, and it wasn't as though such incidents had never taken place before. Hindus and Muslims used to take these things lightly. At worst, if the drunkard had overdone it, he was taken to the police station. We had, however, never seen a drunkard being subjected to such a violent beating. This incident showed us clearly the kind of rift that had been created between Hindus and Muslims.

My younger brother, Shyamal, finished his matriculation,

the year I finished my Intermediate. We both needed to secure college admission. Our results came out in July. Usually, college admission was an easy task. All we had to do was submit the fees and we would get enrolled. But Krishnanagar Government College was the only one in the area and there were a limited number of seats. We were worried that if we were late we wouldn't get a place. But every time we went to the college we heard that nobody would be admitted before 15 August when the country would be divided and India would gain independence.

This, of course, made us nervous. We were very anxious about where Krishnanagar would fall after the partition, whether it would be in India or East Pakistan. In Nadia, Muslims were in the majority, so we were sure that the district would be divided. But we did not know which nation Krishnanagar would fall within. Hindus formed the majority in Krishnanagar, so we thought we would be in India, but it wasn't something we could be certain about.

There were some isolated incidents that had taken place, which made the Hindus worried about the future. These incidents had to do with rowdy Muslim boys passing comments about young Hindu girls, saying things like 'once Pakistan is formed, these girls will belong to us.' Perhaps, they had not really thought of doing anything, but these comments were enough for the guardians of these girls to feel really scared. Some of these people left their towns and migrated to West Bengal. We saw some of these Hindu gentlemen in Krishnanagar, a few had come to the

Congress office and narrated their experiences, which I had an opportunity to hear. As a reaction to these seemingly trivial events, Hindus once again began to make bombs and arm themselves. We saw some familiar faces of the Hindustan National Guard in Krishnanagar and heard that they had come to learn how to use revolvers and grenades.

We had learnt that Cyril Radcliff had submitted his report to Lord Mountbatten. Until the details of the report were published, there was nothing to do but wait and worry. If we had to temporarily live in Pakistan, until the finer contours of the border were decided, it would be a catastrophe. There were only a few days left till 15 August. We couldn't go to college; we couldn't do anything, and this forced sedentary life – a kind of imprisonment – became painful.

When we woke up on 14 August, the first thing I thought was that the next day we would be citizens of a nation that was independent of British rule. Even if that independence would push us towards Pakistan, I would be able to breathe the air of a free country. I was cognizant of the fact that this was coming after many decades of political movements – armed and peaceful – and what separated us from freedom was just one night.

And yet, for all my excitement and happiness, the worry of which side of the border we would end up in remained heavy in our minds. If Krishnanagar was to become a permanent part of East Pakistan after the division, then there were many question marks hanging over our future.

At midnight, I stood in front of a radio shop. There was

a huge crowd. We stood there, all of us, and heard Nehru speak the now famous words – our tryst with destiny – and that's how I knew that power had changed hands, and we were citizens of the new nation of East Pakistan. Nobody felt happy about this. In the crowd, there was a significant number of Muslims, and they didn't look happy either. No firecrackers were burst. The next day, the sun rose in an independent Pakistan. The Pakistan flag was supposed to be raised in the town hall grounds, and I knew I had to go there because I used to hang out with senior members of the Congress in their office and was seen as a 'Congressi type'.

I did not want to be considered as part of the 'enemy' camp, so to speak, now that we were in Pakistan. So, I went there. On the ground, we saw that the Congress president hoisted the flag. Standing behind him were Naseeruddin, the DM, the police superintendent, the newly promoted DIG of East Pakistan and Shamshud Doha, who was notorious for his role in the Calcutta riots the year before. The Muslim League MLA was also there, of course. The flag was hoisted, the Congress leader expressed his commitment to the new nation, and we all shouted slogans of 'Pakistan Zindabad' and 'Quaid-e-Azam Zindabad'. Then the ceremony ended.

Krishnanagar felt like a ghost town. As my friends and I walked its empty streets, I spotted the odd rickshaw or horse cart, and the passengers were usually a couple of men. No women could be spotted anywhere. Previously, in the relatively liberal environment of Krishnanagar, it was a familiar sight to see women on the streets, in groups or by themselves. But on this day, there were none.

We too talked to ourselves in low voices. We didn't feel happy about gaining independence in Pakistan. It was a day spent in sorrow. Schools, offices, colleges, courts were all closed. The cinema was shut. No one was playing football in the fields. The entire town was waiting with bated breath for the Radcliffe report to be made public.

We felt cornered. We were worried about the animosity the Muslims felt towards us. We were scared of the authorities. We were scared of our new rulers in Islamabad. At home, we heard our parents worry about how to start a new life in a new place. If Krishnanagar was to become a permanent part of East Pakistan, then there would have to be some major changes in the household, and I knew my parents were worried about that.

16 August was spent in the same way. But we read some news from Calcutta that gave us some strength. There were some stories of Hindu–Muslim harmony in Calcutta from 14 August. There were small processions of each community that travelled to meet the other and gave them garlands, fed them sweets and initiated hope for a new era of communal harmony. Nobody could imagine that such a thing would happen. And these were just ordinary people. Without caring a hoot about political leaders, they managed to stem the tide of year-long Hindu–Muslim riots in Calcutta. Of course, Gandhiji was a great influence behind this.

It was the same the next day: a day of no real news, a day with the same old worries. Schools, colleges and offices had opened but were not functioning normally. We hoped the fate of Krishnanagar would be decided immediately. At midnight on 18 August, we heard the sounds of firecrackers and conch shells being blown. At first, we thought the riots that were thwarted for so long had started. We were totally disoriented, almost frozen in confusion and fear.

But then we heard Gandhi's name being chanted and Congress leaders being hailed. We saw people were smiling and coming out on the streets, and that's when we realized that Krishnanagar was going to remain a part of India. All the Pakistani flags were brought down. Those who had raised them were the same people who brought them down.

The DM, Naseeruddin, transferred the responsibility to the new magistrate – a Hindu – and left for his new workplace, Kushtia, which had become a part of East Pakistan. Strangers and friends were greeting each other with chants of 'Jai Hind'. It may have been midnight, but the streets were filled with people. Everyone was overwhelmed with emotion by the news.

The newspapers from Calcutta came before daybreak, and they were pounced upon. Even people who didn't usually buy or read the papers almost snatched them from the hands of the hawkers. We read that, irrespective of a Hindu majority, Khulna had become a part of East Pakistan, and Murshidabad, which had a Muslim majority, was part of West Bengal. There was a meeting of all the leaders at the

DM's office, and it was decided that on 19 August a new celebration of attaining independence would take place and that 18 August would be reserved to prepare for this.

The city completely changed that day. Everyone had the flag pinned to their shirts and kurtas, and everyone was smiling. On the morning of 19 August, when I saw the kind of crowds of people on the streets of Krishnanagar, I wondered where these people were on the 17th! There was such a big crowd that one could get lost in it. Everyone was greeting each other with 'Jai Hind', smiling, and shaking hands. I probably shook hands with more than three hundred people that morning.

My throat was sore from singing nationalist songs. The Muslim League MLA hoisted the Indian flag in the town hall ground. The real celebration took place in the evening and continued well into the night. The officials of various clubs delivered speeches. There were cultural programmes, patriotic plays were enacted, songs were sung, and the crowds continued to throng the streets. Nobody went to sleep that night.

———•———

Cyril Radcliffe was the joint chairman of the two boundary commissions that were set up to draw a border in order to carve out a territory for Pakistan. The idea was to demarcate the boundary on the basis of contiguous areas occupied by Muslims and non-Muslims.[2] Of course, other factors were to be taken into consideration too; these included watercourses, irrigation systems, 'natural boundaries', language and dialect, etc. These were vague and gave Radcliffe, who had just five weeks to come up with a new border, enough leeway.

On arriving in India, Radcliffe travelled to Calcutta and Lahore and met with both Nehru and Jinnah. He was not happy about the truncated schedule he was given, but the one thing all parties could agree on was that the new border should be ready by 15 August. Radcliffe did submit his report by the 15th, but because of political considerations and the fear of violence that was already building up and expected to escalate, it was decided that it would be published only on 17 August. For those two days, India and Pakistan were like 'conjoined twins'.[3] In various parts, the border was not defined. Many places raised both Indian and Pakistani flags since they weren't certain on which side they would fall.

It was a difficult assignment imposed upon a reluctant individual. Even so, when the line was published it seemed like an entirely casual division. Radcliffe himself was of the opinion that people would suffer, no matter what he did. He destroyed all his papers before he left India.[4] On 16 August, representatives of India and Pakistan were given two hours to look at the proposal, and they were announced on 17 August. Some rationalization of the line occurred over the next few days.

In December 1947, the West Bengal government organized a public meeting to felicitate Jawaharlal Nehru. I travelled to Calcutta by train in the morning to attend the meeting and hear Nehru's speech. When we reached, we found out that the loudspeakers near the podium were not working properly. The huge crowd that had gathered there on the day was beginning to get upset about the situation. The police had clearly not anticipated such a large gathering, and there were not enough policemen there to control the crowd if things went wrong. When Nehru began his speech, he realized that many in the audience could not hear him properly, were getting agitated and trying to come closer to the podium. There was a stampede and the bamboo barricades that had been put up soon began to break. Not before long, wave upon wave of people began to crash against the podium. The meeting was adjourned so that Nehru could leave the place unharmed. There were no policemen nearby who could create a cordon for a safe passage; a few had probably died during the stampede. Nehru somehow managed to get out safely and go to Raj Bhavan.

I was heartbroken to not be able to hear one of my heroes speak, having made such a long journey to the big city. But little did I know that the following month would bring me bad news of a far more serious kind. I learnt of Gandhi's murder on the evening of 30 January when my classmate Surajmal Somani came home to tell me. I could not believe it, so I went to a sweet shop which had a radio to confirm the news for myself. When I reached, there was already sad music playing, and every five minutes the news of Gandhi's death was repeated. Everybody gathered there was crying. I had never seen such universal grief.

A Muslim tailor from the neighbourhood, who was standing next to me, was desperately asking if it was a Hindu or a Muslim who killed Gandhi, and I could understand why the man was so anxious. I was worried as well. If the killer was Muslim, there was a strong possibility of another massive riot.

Everybody had tears in their eyes, but if Gandhi's killer was a Muslim, then these same people would run after Muslims with whatever they could find in front of them. Then the leaders began to speak. First, there was Nehru's 'The light has gone out of our lives' speech, but the identity of the killer was still unknown. Then Sardar Patel spoke in Hindi and he said that, 'Ek Hindu naujawan ne unko mara' (A young Hindu man assassinated him). There was a palpable sense of relief amongst the crowd. I had no intention of listening to the news any more and started back for home.

Most shops were shut; there were hundreds of people on the road and people were crying. I hadn't really fathomed the reverence and respect that people had for Gandhi in their hearts till that time. I still remember the way *Anandabazar Patrika* and the English newspaper *Hindustan Standard* reported the death on 31 January and 1 February. It was extremely reserved and tasteful. The entire front page was white, and on the edit page there was a black border on one side and only a few words written in a large font that epitomized the deep emptiness and despair of the entire nation. On these two days, there were no advertisements printed in these newspapers. I was bereft. We were all in shock.

The euphoria of independence seemed to die down after Gandhi's assassination. The times were hard, and it was difficult to be hopeful about the future. There were also many attempts to create communal disturbances all across West Bengal. There was no work, and the future looked bleak. The thought of our impending unemployment and the possibility of starvation made all of us despondent. To console ourselves, we would meet at Momin Park in Krishnanagar and pass the time telling tall tales to each other.

2

A Reality Check

Ambika Menon was born in 1936 in Palakkad, Kerala. She worked as a teacher and a gender researcher. She now lives in Kochi.

I was born in Palakkad in Kerala on 16 April 1936. I am the eldest, and I have one brother who is very close to me in age and another, who is much younger. When I was born, my father was the headmaster of the municipal high school in Ooty. I spent my first two years between Palakkad and Ooty. In 1937, my father got a job in Doon School in Dehradun and he moved there. My brother was born during that time, so my grandmother kept my mother and us children in Palakkad. Mother had not been too well, in that she briefly had post natal depression. This played into my grandmother's hands. My grandmother did not believe in allopathy and insisted on Ayurvedic treatment, a long process with strict diet schedules and sleep routines. Further, the treatment had to be done three years in a row. My father, anxious about mother's health, agreed, despite his longing to be reunited with his wife and children.

Mother's well-being was his primary concern and for that he would make any sacrifices throughout his life. He came down for both the holidays twice a year, a five-day journey each way.

We finally joined my father in Dehradun when I was about four, but we used to come to Palakkad during the holidays every year.

On one of those holidays, my grandmother said she was worried about being separated from us during wartime and made us stay. She didn't want to part from her daughter, basically. And so, she made one excuse or the other to keep us with her. She insisted that to look after two small children would be too much of a burden for my mother, which was true. My mother, poor thing, was torn between her mother's insistence and her own inclination to be with her husband.

My father was deeply concerned about our schooling and spent much time playing educational games with us through his vacation. Together, they invented a host of activities for us to keep our minds alert. Most of all, father wanted our little family to be united. Eventually, mother prevailed upon my grandmother and we travelled to Dehradun taking a maid per child along with us – it was quite a caravan.

The freedom movement was a strong presence in my childhood. In Kerala, the vernacular press – *Mathrubhumi* and *Manorama* – play a huge part in the state's readership.

Mathrubhumi was very much on the ascendant during the freedom movement. A founding member of that paper was one of our karnavaurs (senior, male member of the family), a first cousin of my grandmother, in fact.

In most tharavads (Kerala family homes), *Mathrubhumi* was a staple. Once the newspaper was delivered in my house, it was distributed page by page to various members. I remember my mother's brothers and other uncles sitting on the front stoop, in what was called in Kerala 'easy chairs', reading the papers and engaging in huge discussions with each other.

There were long, passionate arguments about all the important topics of the day. Often there were critiques of the movement. You couldn't help but hear these. All the great heroes – Gandhi, Nehru, Patel – were household names for my brother and me. It must have been the same for many kids during that time.

The *Mathrubhumi* connection meant that as a family we had an involvement with journalism and the Congress. Then, there was my father's brother who disappeared in Malaysia and joined the INA with Subhas Chandra Bose. One of my mother's brothers, who did not want to study, ran away and joined the British Army during the Second World War. Therefore, there was an involvement with the Congress, with the INA and the British Army.

The freedom movement was an intrinsic part of our household and our lives. Many homes had the same sort of mix. Certainly the armed forces (navy or army), the Congress and the freedom movement were part of most families. My family members were dyed-in-the-wool Congress supporters, of course. There is a very famous photograph of Nehru and Gandhi, heads close to each other, taken by the renowned photographer Margaret Bourke-White. That photo used to hang over the entrance door to our house. To this day, the picture is imprinted on my mind.

Our tharavad is originally in Malappuram. But my mother's uncles – that is, two generations before me – built the house in Palakkad in order to pursue English education. This home allowed the family to go to convent or mission schools in Palakkad town and then to Victoria College. By that time, you couldn't get a job without English.

I went to a school in Palakkad for one day. My mother enrolled me in a German mission school, one which she herself had attended. It was called Moyan Girls High School. I went for one day, and my brother absolutely refused. To accommodate his determined refusal and because our parents did not wish to separate us, I, too, was withdrawn from the school. My father was very concerned about my brother and me getting a proper education and appointed what might be called a day governess.

All the railway staff in those days used to be – how do I put it – people who could not make it to other, more important, services. There was a family there, the stationmaster and his daughter. Her name was Daphne Burgess.

She was hired to teach us. Actually, she spent the morning with us. She was not used to sitting on the floor and eating, nor was she accustomed to vegetarian food, which was the only food that was cooked in the house. Maybe my grandmother too did not want her to eat in our home, I don't know. Whatever it was, she didn't eat with us and went home at lunchtime.

My father had sent us a lot of books. There was a series called *The Songs the Letters Sing*, another called *Pet Family and Lands and Lives*. She taught us from there or took us for a walk in our big backyard and garden where she would teach us the names of trees, plants and flowers. She knew a little poetry and could recite poems about a flower or a cloud or whatever. Daphne Burgess could be credited for our interest in poetry too. (*Laughs.*) That was how I started my education.

I was nine and my brother was nearly eight when we finally came to Dehradun once the war ended in 1945. By then, anticipation was building in Kerala about the British exiting India. There was a feeling in the air that we would be free soon. But when we went to Dehradun and entered the campus of a British public school, it was a completely different atmosphere.

In those days, all senior masters in Doon School were British, and among the teachers, my father was the first person they had hired who didn't have a degree from a British university. He was from Presidency College, Madras. On the campus, there was a distinction between the British masters and the Indian masters, not in behaviour or in the way they engaged with each other, but in terms of salaries. The British teachers were better paid than their Indian counterparts.

They had various allowances which the Indian masters did not. By the time we got there in 1945 probably half the teachers were Indians. Many of the British teachers had left during the war years. Some joined the armed forces; others participated in the war efforts in other ways.

Strangely, in my nine-year-old head I made a distinction between the British who I interacted with on a daily basis – people who were warm, concerned and caring – and the British who ruled the country and who the Congress was fighting. We roamed the campus freely. People would invite us for chocolate or a treat of some kind. In my head, there was no conflict because of these distinctions I had made. It was a very friendly atmosphere. I never felt there was any racism on that campus.

The irony was that neither my brother nor I, despite hanging out with Daphne Burgess, could speak English. The headmaster's wife had a little group of assorted kids who she would teach. She also employed an army officer's wife, a British lady, as a teacher. This was where I first went to school in Dehradun. Here, I picked up the rudiments of English.

After about two years, my parents put me in a convent. They tested me, found me wanting in English and put me in Class 2. The next day, they put me in Class 3, and so on, and – within a fortnight – I reached Class 5.

Amazingly, it had no impact on me that I can remember. I cannot recall feeling belittled by being in a class where the children were much younger than me. I had no experience of a school before. I was used to studying with a motley bunch of kids. I had been in the convent barely three months or less when the pre-Partition riots broke out. It was unsafe for children to be sent to school, so all schools in the area shut down. And I thought it was Christmas!

To pass my time, I began to play tennis with the head groundsman on the Doon campus. Every Wednesday, they had a masters' meeting called Chambers. Once, the headmaster, on his way to the Chambers, walked past the tennis court and saw me. I saw him standing and watching and then carrying on. I thought nothing of it. But apparently, after the meeting, he called my father and said, 'Nair, what is Ambika doing in the tennis court? Shouldn't she be in school?'

So my father said, 'Yes, but the convent is closed, and there is no school for her. It's better she is on the tennis courts rather than wasting her time.' The headmaster was a very taciturn person. He didn't say anything to that. But he came up to my father later in the day and said, 'Nair, suppose I put it to the board of governors that Ambika be allowed to attend classes in school, would you be willing to let her?' My father said he would be delighted.

Of course, no one asks kids their opinion on these things. That weekend, there was a board of governors meeting in Delhi where the proposal was put toward. The board said yes, although they warned him that it would be a challenge to manage one girl amidst so many boys. The headmaster came back and told my father that the board had passed his proposal. My father informed me that I could start school with the boys. That was how I became the first girl to attend Doon School.

By then, a lot of things were happening. Independence was announced, and speculation about Partition was rife. Every summer, we went down to Kerala because my father got almost three months' vacation. It was towards the end of our time in Kerala in 1947 that the Partition riots intensified. We had a lot of trouble coming back to Dehradun. There was a total rerouting of the train, the Grand Trunk Express, and they had to avoid all areas with a Muslim majority. We took a very circuitous route. I am not sure, but I think it was partly by bus and partly by train. I know we ended up in Mysore, and from there we came to Dehradun. This was August 1947.

We lived in a bungalow outside the campus. It was across the road. Behind us was a slope, which went down to a riverbed. For a couple of weeks, throughout the nights, we were hearing chants of 'Har Har Mahadev' and 'Allah hu Akbar'. This was not the independence we had envisioned. It didn't frighten us because (and I speak on behalf of my brother too; he has passed away, unfortunately, but at the time we shared a room and were very much with each other) we were certain that our parents would protect us from any danger.

We were concerned because for the first time we had encountered death. Yes, we knew death was inevitable, but we had never seen it up close. On campus, every boarding house had a resident tailor. The tailor who worked in the hostel that my father was in charge of was a Muslim. It happened to be a Friday, and all of us knew that Friday was special for Muslims and there was no way they would miss the namaz. The tailor got ready and he did his wazu and all that.

He told my mother, 'I'm just going down to the mosque to say my prayer.' My mother begged him. She said, 'Please don't go. It's dangerous. Say your namaz here. If you like, I will sweep and wipe the floor for you and there is a brand-new, unwashed bedcover. Please spread that and say your namaz. Nobody will disturb you.' But he said, 'Nahin memsaab, don't worry. Allah will look after me.' And he went out, and he was killed! He never came back. To this day, that picture of the veranda where he sat with his Singer sewing machine, to which no tailor came back, is one of the photographs in my memory.

I couldn't comprehend what this communal killing was. The tailor had done nothing. He was a gentle, elderly man. In what way had he harmed anyone? Yes, we grew up with the war. War is a fight between two armies; it has its own rules. But this was different. This was a person walking on the streets who was senselessly killed. That confused us a great deal.

While I will not say the incident took away our joy at the news of independence, it certainly coloured it. There were two streams. One was of elation that Gandhiji and his movement had accomplished what they set out to achieve and now it was for the Congress, minus Gandhi, to carry it forward. At the same time, there was the sense of pity for a nation fighting itself. Gandhi, Nehru, Patel were all loudly opposing the riots and trying to calm people down.

For the first time, on 14 August, my brother and I were allowed to stay up till midnight to listen to Nehru's speech. We stood on either side of the radio and wept. Both of us. (*Laughs.*) I don't know why. We weren't sobbing, but tears kept flowing from our eyes. Then a very sombre eleven- and ten-year-old went to bed.

The next day carried none of this ambivalence. The school held a flag hoisting ceremony. 'Jana Gana Mana' happened to be the first song in our prayer book. Since Doon School had started in 1935, that song had always been sung at our assemblies. All of us knew it, so we were gathered and we sang. The British masters were there, the Indian masters were there, and so were all the families. I think, if it's not a colouring of my imagination, laddoos were distributed.

Wait a minute! Actually, I don't remember what we did at all. I think this was perhaps an assumption my brain has made about what happened on the first Independence Day, based on the rituals of subsequent years. I can't really say what had happened at school on 15 August 1947. Independence itself was a continuum of the freedom struggle and the riots took precedence. Our overwhelming emotion was not elation. It was grief.

In the following days, life carried on as usual. The events outside did have a resonance, but not a lot because we were living on a campus. Besides, boarding schools have to be running on a schedule, from the time you wake up to the time you go to sleep. Otherwise, you can't manage the children. Therefore, we didn't have much time.

Besides, Independence Day was not independent of life as such. We saw the whole thing as a movement – and ever since my brother and I became aware, we had been caught up in it. We also picked up the adults' anxiety about how much further we had to go to get India back on its feet.

We knew Nehru and his cabinet faced a huge challenge. We had no concept of politics or governance, but we knew it would be tough to deal with the poverty and the deprivation. We had all heard about the Bengal famine. Thanks to the vernacular press, in fact. We knew how much the British had exploited us. Also, as landowners in Kerala, we knew how much of the harvest they took. What we should have got by right, we only got a small percentage of. And this was true for everybody. Independence Day was not a goal but a milestone.

The British masters started leaving the school and going back to Britain over the next few years. But two opted to stay back and, in fact, they lived the rest of their lives in India, one in Ajmer and the other in Dehradun. We felt a sense of inevitability about these departures. I didn't have any value judgements, but I was also happy that the two who opted to stay, stayed. The one in Dehradun I would meet often even later in my life. The one in Ajmer I didn't get many opportunities to visit.

I always felt this was my country. I saw the British as intruders. They claimed overlordship but India was India. Being from Kerala helped because at that time the state had kept its culture. There was nothing westernized about most homes there. The notion that this was our country, this was our home, was really easy to internalize. What troubled me was the question of where would we end this division of the country. Even as an eleven-year-old I wondered whether all Muslims were going to shift to Pakistan. Were all Hindus coming to India? How would that work? I don't think I knew enough at the time. This is probably more in hindsight. We had conversations about this at home, I remember, and my parents were reassuring. We had very good Muslim friends. They used to point out that they were not going to Pakistan. That it was not compulsory for all Muslims to go, but that it was an option, and people could stay where they wanted. They said both nations would continue as mixed nations. At least that's what they expected then.

I had heard about Jinnah. What I overheard as a child, and the colouring I put on it was, what I now think of as an ego clash, and what I thought then was a personal clash between Nehru and Jinnah as to who would succeed Gandhi as the leader. That was my perception of it as a child. When it came to Jinnah, what seemed to concern most people was why he was demanding Pakistan.

What was anyone gaining from it? What was he gaining from dividing the country? Jinnah himself hadn't been known to say namaz. He was not a practising Muslim. He was very much a westernized person. When he couldn't get Gandhi's support or assurance that he would be his successor, he decided to create that spot for himself. That was a personal power play on his part and not led by his ideology. This was my feeling.

I remember an incident that happened after independence. Jawaharlal Nehru used to come to Dehradun very often. He loved the circuit house there. The security provision there was a hedge around the building and not even a wall! He came often for weekends or whenever he could take a break or needed some quiet. The way he would arrive was astounding. I actually passed one of his convoys on the road once. There was a car in front, which I imagine was a security car. Then there was his vehicle, I think it was an Ambassador. This was followed by a first-aid van and a jeep. A siren went off once in a while. He used to have four motorcycle outriders. Two in front of the convoy and two at the back. And that was the sum total of the security apparatus of the prime minister of India, travelling during one of the most troubled times in the country's history.

He could have easily been a target. It was the same when he visited the refugee camps. There was hardly any security. Once, he visited the school. He was walking down, and we were all charmed by this man. There was no greater hero for us. I remember, I sidled up to him and poked him with my finger. I wanted to see if he was for real! What cheek. (*Laughs.*) What cheek for a little girl to go and poke the prime minister of India, checking if he was real or just a figure on a grainy film!

Doon School was modelled on British public schools, especially Harrow and Eton, but it wasn't Western in any way. The prayers were Indian. Rabindranath Tagore was involved with the school early on; the music master and art master came from Santiniketan. There was an emphasis on 'Indian'. The atmosphere in the school was that of very privileged Indians who got a chance to be taken for what they were and not looked down as being colonized.

I ended up studying there for six years. I didn't go back to the convent because they wanted to try this as an experiment. A year later, the other masters asked why couldn't their daughters join? Then it became a rule that masters' daughters could attend Doon. That rule still stands.

Being the only girl in school was hard. Boys, for fear of being teased, kept their distance from me, and I kept my distance from them. In effect, I made no friends. The only time we may have chit-chatted was when we were acting together, or during debates or declamations. Otherwise, there was no conversation. I don't have any friends from my schooldays. My oldest friends are from the convent I attended, even though I was there for such a short time. From Doon School, I have a lot of acquaintances, and I still keep up with them. There are only seven of us from our batch left now. We are, sort of, in touch.

After I finished school, my one dream was to become a doctor, as it had always been ever since I remember. I never considered being anything else. But my grandmother said no. Mothers' mothers had a lot of clout in our community in those days. She said she wanted me to get married since I was the only girl in the family. She said, 'I know her and if she takes medicine, she won't get married, and we won't have any successors.'

I found this very annoying. My father was quite helpless because my mother was torn between my desire for medicine and my grandmother's wishes. She knew how much becoming a doctor meant to me. But her mother was threatening to commit suicide if I went ahead! It got very dramatic. She said she would hang herself if I took admission. My parents sat me down and said, 'This is the situation. What would you like to do?' I said, 'I don't want to harass you.'

I had no interest in feminine activities. I had studied carpentry and metalwork, not sewing and embroidery. I said if marriage was my goal, I should prepare for it. I decided to go to Lady Irwin College in Delhi and study BSc Home Science. This lasted all of three months because I picked up some amoebiasis and other health issues. When my father came to see me in October I was so frail that he said, 'I am not letting you stay here.' He took me back.

He was worried that I had completely lost interest in what I was doing because I wasn't allowed to study medicine. I still hoped that I could persuade my grandmother to change her mind. I took up BSc Zoology hoping that I could change to medicine. It didn't work. But by this point, a little more distance had come between my deep disappointment and me, and so I thought, well, if I am not going to be able to do what I really want to do, I might as well learn subjects I really liked. So, I went to Lucknow to Isabella Thoburn College and studied geography and philosophy. Interestingly, my local guardian in Lucknow, who was a friend of my parents, was closely associated with some prominent Congress people in the city.

I enjoyed the two years in Lucknow – it was a real lark. The city had a syncretic culture. There was no fear of violence as there was at the time of independence. I was in a happy and hopeful state of mind. I remember a few of us girls going to watch the Muharram procession. And it was quite all right for us to do that. Whereas today I doubt it would be.

After that, I did my MA. I got a scholarship in Lucknow University, but they did not have a hostel for girls. I would have had to stay with my parents' friends, which I didn't fancy. I had also got admission in Miranda House, and so I came to Delhi for my MA in philosophy. The philosophy department was a mess when I joined.

My interest was Buddhism, but they had no professors for that subject. The college itself was going through an upheaval. I spent more time at the Russian and Chinese embassy protesting because the invasion of Hungary and the trouble in Tibet had taken place at that time. Then, I got a wire from the headmaster of Doon School saying, 'If you aren't planning to finish your MA, come immediately and join the staff here.' In 1957, I went back to Dehradun and became the geography teacher at Doon School.

My job at Doon was not a permanent position. But at that time, the Welham Girls' School was just starting. They were looking for staff. The headmaster of Doon School was on their board, and he asked me if I would like to join there.

I said yes. There were thirteen students in the first batch at Welham. Subhashini Ali and Brinda Karat, both of who went on to become stalwarts in the Communist Party of India, were among my charges.

There I was, earning a salary and having my own set of friends. In those days, it was a heady experience for a young woman. I was perhaps twenty-one or so. Then my parents asked me to come home and stay with them. I got a job close by in another school in Dehradun, which was walking distance from the house my parents lived in. Back then, it was very easy to get a teaching job. And that's where I stayed till I got married. I did not resent having to leave Welham to live with my parents. I was quite content.

Mine was very much an arranged marriage. There were a lot of discussions and many prospective grooms. I kept shooting each one down till I was twenty-three, which in that era was ancient. At this stage I talked to myself and said, I know nothing about the guy I am going to marry, so it is better to just let my parents decide. I had this strange feeling that I could make it work. But I must also tell you that I did not make it work! My husband and I separated. That was thirty-two years after we got married, but there were many times in between that I left, and he would come and apologize, and we would try and make another go of it.

My husband had a good job. He was based in Rourkela. What I saw in Orissa coloured my subsequent life. I saw the displacement of tribals, and it troubled me so deeply that I said to myself, at some point, I am going to come back here and work with them. And I did. In my marriage, we moved around quite a bit; we were in Jamshedpur, Bombay, Delhi. Six years after my marriage, I had a son and later, two daughters. I was quite fine, even if not entirely happy.

There was a degree of independence that I enjoyed. I had friends; I had access to things I liked; I could swim; I could go to the club and play tennis. But what my husband would not let me do was take up a job. He felt my job would be a blot on his status and position. He said it would make it awkward because his customers were top executives, and they would look down on me on account of my job. He gave me very 'good' reasons, and I bought them.

The country was rolling along. As long as Pandit Nehru was prime minister – and he did many things wrong which I recognized as wrong even at that time – I always had hope for the country because there was decency. But when he gave Indira Gandhi the space to seek a position of power, I think he made his biggest mistake.

I supported her overtly in the initial years. In our social gatherings, the men would always pooh-pooh her and mock her for her squeaky voice and convent diction. I used to get annoyed that these men couldn't accept the fact that a woman was prime minister. There were huge arguments where I stood up for her, without actually liking her. Of course, there were things she did right too. My dislike for her shouldn't colour her good decisions.

She never made us feel that the Indian prime minister was less than the Western leaders. This was something that

Nehru too had practised. He was as good as anybody. Indira Gandhi stood up to Richard Nixon, to Henry Kissinger. But when she started this cult of her sons, I completely lost faith in her. This country has a lot of potential; it doesn't have to find every prime minister from that family.

I was hoping that there would be a churn in the Congress, at least after Rajiv Gandhi's assassination. But with Sonia stepping in, it just did not happen. And it isn't going to happen now, unless the family withdraws from the party. I don't think anyone can generate enough drum swell except the Congress, and I am saying this as someone who is not a Congress voter. They have the local ground staff for it. It's unfortunate that they are literally killing the party.

Was it Churchill who said that India is a functioning anarchy? [It was John Kenneth Galbraith.] The BJP made that come true. This is where I get annoyed with Sonia Gandhi. I thought Manmohan Singh did a good job, but he was given neither the space to do what he wanted, nor the credit for things he did. It was always about what Sonia Gandhi wanted. And I don't agree with all these theories about her sacrifice of the prime ministership.

I don't think she was qualified to become the prime minister. If you recall the pictures from that time, the Gandhi family had such glum faces before it was announced that Manmohan Singh would head the government. I think she would have loved play that role. And all the while, the Congress kept going down.

I feel that it isn't that the BJP won in 2014 but that the

Congress gave India to them. There was such a sense of hopelessness that the BJP's rhetoric found an audience. I was hoping that, perhaps, it would be like A.B. Vajpayee's kind of leadership. After 2014, I still held out hope.

Now, this sort of lumpen street violence, the business of lynching and such, it bothers me much more than politics. It's just not Indian, that ethos, and to be very, very clear, it's not Hindu. Hinduism is inclusive – it has stood the test of time, and there has been no danger to Hinduism until the defenders of the religion came to power. I am a practising Hindu. I don't believe in rituals. But I do believe in Indian philosophy. And what is happening in this country now, is completely against it. That bothers me.

How has the female experience of the country evolved? I have never felt different, to the extent that my parents brought us up very equally. My brother and I had similar rules. Except for the fact that he could go trekking and I couldn't because I didn't have the right escort. But I could swim, go on cycling picnics and play tennis, squash and whatever. They never stopped me from doing what I wanted. Except, pursue medicine, of course. And they did not stop me; they were cornered. I did not rebel though I recognized that my grandmother's threat was just a bluff. It continues to mystify me. Medicine was not an overwhelming interest or a career choice. It was a passion.

So, really, I have never felt restricted because I am a woman. I have only felt that I was restricted because I hadn't made enough of an effort to break out. Also, when I was growing up, there were so many examples of women who were active in public life, especially in the Congress movement, whom I knew. There were women in the forefront, marching, there were activists. A great heroine of mine was Sarojini Naidu. There were other stellar examples too, like Lakshmi Sahgal, Ammu Swaminathan, etc. These were great role models for us. Eventually, I worked on gender issues in the development sector. That taught me a lot.

———— ● ————

Ammu Swaminathan was a political activist and a social worker. She was a follower of Gandhiji and served as a member of the Constituent Assembly of India, after independence. Later, she became a Rajya Sabha member. In 1975, on the inauguration of the International Women's Year, she was selected as the 'Mother of the Year'.[1]

Part of what contributed to her 'Mother of the Year' award were the accomplishments of her daughter, Lakshmi Sahgal, who too was an active participant in the independence movement. She was an officer in the Indian National Army. She met Subhas Chandra Bose and set up an all-women's regiment in the INA called the Rani of Jhansi Regiment. She was arrested by the British in Burma in 1945 and returned to India in 1946.[2]

———— ● ————

When I was younger, I was pretty clear about my career being a hobby, because my first job was always to be there for my children. Everything worked around that. If I took up a job, I would make sure that I left the house after my children left for school, and I would be back home before they returned. And that I would be home during their holidays. So that is why I went into teaching. I did my gender activism after my children grew up and left home. I went back to Orissa, in fact! For a long time, I had told my husband that when he retired that was what I would want to do – go back to Orissa and work with the tribal population. I don't think he ever took that seriously. But I did. I was certain that I was going to do it. And finally, I did.

I left my husband, went to a small tribal village called Mahura, which is near Berhampur. I lived and worked with the people there. I was there for five years. After that, I wandered like a nomad. I had no home; my mother's brothers had wrecked the family home and fortunes.

I moved from Orissa to Lucknow to Delhi, working with various NGOs and other organizations, on projects related to gender. I had no address. It was an amazing experience. When I walked out of my marriage for the last time, I had two medium-sized Samsonite suitcases and a small carton of books. That was all I had. This was after having lived a substantial life. I don't know if it was brave, but it was certainly what I wanted to do. It was a lovely experience. I had never been happier in my life.

3

Rising up in Rouse Avenue

Ved Prakash Malhotra was born in Lahore in 1939. He lives in Delhi with his wife. He spent most of his working life in the USAID. He has two sons.

I was born in Lahore in undivided India on 4 March 1939. My father was working with the People's Bank in Lahore. We lived in a big bungalow in the city in a place called Gawalmandi, which is very famous now. I saw some photos of the neighbourhood recently. We were a joint family; all my uncles lived with us. It was a four-room set. I remember we even had a buffalo in our courtyard at the back. In fact, I remember this clearly because I once fell down from the balcony on to the buffalo!

When I was a child, I was the only boy in the whole family. My grandmother was very fond of me. The house was L-shaped. My grandmother used to call me secretly and we would hide on the other side of the L, and she would feed me fresh cream from the buffalo milk mixed with sugar. I remember her looking behind to make sure that no one saw us. At the time, special attention was given to boys.

For a part of my childhood we stayed in a district called Jhang. My grandfather was a big landlord, and he was very rich. In the house was a big, dark room, and in the centre was a trunk filled with coins.

My grandfather was a very kind-hearted man. If a poor person came and asked for help, he would take fistfuls of coins from the trunk and give them the money. We had a lot of fields, and about ten or fifteen people used to work in the fields. I spent quite some time there before we moved to Lahore.

My grandfather married twice, both times to women called Parvati. His first wife died in a year. One day, his second wife bought a beautiful shawl and gifted it to her husband. She had gone to great lengths to procure it. It was specially woven for him. That same day, my grandfather went to a dharamshala. There he saw a poor person. Immediately, he took the shawl off and gave it to him. I was told that there was a great row about that. My grandmother was really angry about it. (*Laughs.*)

When my grandfather died, there was a big crowd. I have a photograph from that time. But the thing was, when he died we realized there was no money left. He had given most of it away. My father worked hard, and then he took the family with him to Lahore. They were ten siblings.

In 1946, when I was seven, my father was transferred from Lahore to Delhi. Do you see how lucky we were?

At that time, there was no talk of Partition. We came to Daryaganj and stayed there for a few months. Then we moved to Rouse Avenue in central Delhi. By we I mean just my father, mother and my two siblings. The rest of the family was still in Lahore. I have five siblings, four brothers and one sister. I was the eldest. Three of us were born in Lahore and three were born here in Delhi. I was in school in Lahore, in Class 1, when we moved to Delhi.

There was a break in my schooling when we moved to Delhi. I was home for six months or so. The first school I joined in Delhi was located on Ranjeet Singh Road. I studied there in Classes 1 and 2. It was an Urdu-medium school. The rent for our Rouse Avenue house was just fifteen rupees! And for us it was a strange experience because it was the first time we were living as a nuclear family.

The first few months were nice, and we were settling down. Then, slowly, as 1947 rolled in, news of small riots and clashes between Hindus and Muslims started trickling in. Then it began to get more severe and more frequent once speculations about a separate country for Muslims started. My father had a strong gut feel that things were going to get really bad. He wrote to the family in Lahore.

'Consider this letter a telegram,' he said. 'Do not wait to see how things unfold. Leave immediately,' he urged them. Since he was the eldest and had considerable power and respect within the family, his brothers listened to him. They packed up whatever little they could – some gold ornaments, not much – and immediately left Lahore. This was probably a week or ten days before the horrific riots and murders began.

Fortunately for us, they arrived here safely. But the same was not true for some members of our extended family. The riots had begun on both sides of the border, even though there was no border! These uncles and cousins witnessed unbelievable horrors. They came riding on the top of trains, while inside the compartment were thousands of dead bodies.

There was another part of the family in Sialkot. My bua's husband was a numberdar, who is some sort of a zamindar. The Muslims there came after him, threatening to kill him and his family. One of his friends, who was also a Muslim, wanted to save him. He told my uncle to hand over the title deed of his land, write it in his name and he would ensure them a safe passage to the other side of the border. My uncle immediately wrote off all his land and possessions, packed a small bag and left with his family. Groups of people chased after them with swords, but the friend kept his word and escorted them safely out of Pakistan.

Most of our family came to us in Rouse Avenue when they reached India. For many years, we all stayed there. Initially, everyone crammed together in a single-bedroom house. At one point there were about ten or fifteen of us. Most of us would have to sleep outdoors, on the roof. Slowly, some people moved to other homes on the same street. The riots continued in Delhi. I remember seeing my uncle chasing a Muslim man. He had apparently killed two or three Hindus.

A mob was chasing him to exact revenge, and my uncle was a part of the mob. I too followed them. Near Bengali Market, the man jumped and hid behind a kothi (bungalow). The mob vanished, but I and a bunch of other kids hung around. In a short while, some five or six people came. They smoked him out of the kothi and beat him to death. I saw this with my own eyes. It was terrifying, but it had also become increasingly common to see things like this.

Even in the locality where we were living, all night we would hear the sounds of Muslims who were leaving their homes and making their way to the railway station to go across the border. The Jan Sangh folks were very active then. At night, there were groups of men who would walk around and guard the place. There were Sikh and Hindu groups. They also used to shout slogans sometimes.

Cries of 'Jai Mahadev' and 'Bole So Nihaal' rang out all night. These people were guarding the area, and the police were not around. The women used to huddle together on the roofs all night. If anyone tried to enter the house downstairs, they were instructed to throw chilli powder on them. The atmosphere was extremely tense, and we were all terrified for our lives.

Our only goal those days was to try and stay safe. Around this time, Mahatma Gandhi had gone around saying 'no Muslims should be harmed'. He had visited our area too. Things were peaceful for two or three days after his visit. Then the killings resumed.

We used to stay awake all night, even though I was only seven. Schools were shut. We used to hear that Jinnah wanted to become the prime minister and Nehru didn't want that. And that's why the country was partitioned. We didn't know who to trust.

Connaught Place, which was the commercial centre of the city and close to us, used to shut at 7 p.m. People would loot the shops there in the dark. There was utter lawlessness. I remember, one of my friends who was nine or ten years old at the time went with his father and looted a tie shop. He asked me to buy a tie from him the next day. (*Laughs.*)

What use did I have for a tie? I asked him where he got it from, and he told me he went 'shopping' with his father the previous night. There used to be wolves at the ridge then. All night, we could hear them howl. The streets were empty after 7 p.m. because anything that moved could kill you. It was utter chaos. Freedom did not feel very freeing.

By 15 August, the murders had been going on relentlessly. There were stories of trains coming from Pakistan that were full of dead bodies on board. People on this side started doing the same. A vengeful attitude had set in. We were all huddled together at home. My father was very strict, and he didn't allow us to step out.

Even though we were in Delhi, in the capital, a stone's throw away from the centre of power, I don't think we even knew that independence had been declared. We heard later that Nehru had made a speech. No one had a radio; we barely had the clothes on our backs and a few pieces of jewellery that the people managed to bring with them.

———————●———————

Jawaharlal Nehru raised the Indian national flag above the Lahori Gate of the Red Fort in Delhi on 15 August 1947, merely five kilometres from Rouse Avenue. India's last Viceroy, Lord Mountbatten, was on the dais with him. By all accounts, this was a crowded affair. *The Times of India* reported the events in Delhi on 15 August 1947 thus:

> Entire Delhi kept awake to witness the historic event of ushering in the freedom of India at the hour of midnight. Unprecedented scenes of enthusiasm were witnessed both inside and outside the Constitution Assembly chamber, where seething, swaying humanity wildly cheered the momentous event, heralded with the blowing of conches.
>
> Raising to the height of the occasion, Pandit Nehru made a speech to the Assembly which was at once notable and a masterpiece of literature.[1]

———

Meanwhile in Bombay:

> A strong police guard kept order with the greatest difficulty till the conclusion of the ceremony when

they lost control and hundreds swarmed through the Building in wild enthusiasm. Their spirit was that of the hundreds of thousands who marched cheering through the illuminated streets of Bombay, uninterruptedly shoutiong slogans in a multitude of tongues, which turned the city at midnight into a Babel.

Bombay in the early hours of Friday morning was a pedestrians' paradise. Cars either drove on the pavements, if they got the right of way, or were marooned there. Rejoicing crowds held the streets and all traffic rules were ignored. Trams and buses were not only packed to doors but carried passengers on their roofs. Everyone cheered as the spirit of the occasion spread infectiously through the city. And few slept as bands blared and trumpets sounded in wild cacophony throughout the memorable night.[2]

———●———

Most people who came from across the border stayed in refugee camps. That is those who didn't have families here. People donated food and clothes. No one could bring anything much with them. One of our relatives, my cousin, got married in the camp. My father went there to bless them. The idea was that this way the girl would be protected. All decisions were based only on one consideration – safety. It is impossible for people who weren't there to understand this psychology. You had to be there.

Our education was interrupted for quite some time, probably close to a couple of years. The first school I was admitted to was destroyed in the riots. Our principal was a Muslim, and the school was a target. I still remember the prayer he taught us, 'Lab pe aati hai dua banke tamanna meri, O Allah!' (May longing come to my lips as supplication of mine, O Allah!). They destroyed the school; nothing remained. I don't remember exactly how long I spent at home. I guess it was more than a year. It would take till 1948–49 for things to improve somewhat.

Soon after independence, my father left the bank. Then, for a while, he worked for a private company. After that he got a job at the US embassy. When he came from Pakistan, my father was only an Intermediate pass. He worked as a book keeper in the private company and there he got a hankering for education.

He signed up for night classes at Camp College. Remember, he was a man with six children by then. Camp College was a tented college where all the refugees used to come to study. During the day, it was a playground. In the evening, it became a college. My father worked all day and went there to do his BA. He used to sleep there too, often, and came home once a week.

After he finished his BA, he started studying for LLB at the same place. And then an MA and an LLM! He did two MAs – in political science and then economics. After that, he started studying Sanskrit. He had a great fondness for learning new things. The family was big and close, so my mother was all right with him spending so much time away from home.

For me, life was very simple. There was no pollution and Delhi was green back then. People used to sleep outside. We had very little money, but we ate pure ghee and drank milk. It was a happy life. My mother was a big influence on me.

My father worked for the joint family. But it was my mother who did all the work for our family. We didn't have much political influence. There was Congress and the Jan Sangh. The only reason to align with a political group was for protection. For a while, I used to go to the Jan Sangh shakha. At the time, it was not a political organization, but a social one. They used to take us on three-day camps and teach us all kinds of things. I admired their discipline. I went to the shakha for a few days. But then I discontinued for various reasons.

I grew up, became a teenager and reached the end of my school life. We had only two options, science or arts. I chose arts. When I was in Class 10, I started giving tuitions to support my family financially. There was an under secretary in the government who lived in Connaught Place. I used to teach his wife English, although my own grasp of the language was not very good. At home, I used to teach myself first, and then I used to go and teach this lady. (*Laughs.*) Luckily, she passed the exams. She even gave me a gift.

After school, I started to learn typing. Some shorthand too. I got a job in the CSIR after giving a typing test. I was not even twenty years old. My main aim was to support my father. He was responsible not just for his wife and children but also his brothers and sisters.

My father secured a job for his younger brother, my uncle, in USAID. After working in Delhi for some time, he was transferred to Kandahar in Afghanistan. So, his post in Delhi became vacant, and my father helped me get it. I was an administrative assistant. I worked in USAID for a long time. After fifteen years, I was laid off when they started reducing their staff in India in the 1970s.

Then, I started working for private companies. After that, surprisingly, there was a job in USAID again. A friend called me and asked if I wanted to return there. I told him, yes, I did. He asked me to rush and fill in the application. In those days, we needed to fill paper applications. The following day was the deadline. I went there, filled the application and gave it to him. Luckily, I got selected. And so, I rejoined the place and worked there until my retirement in March 1999.

I was twenty-eight years old when I got married. Like my father, I too went to college after my marriage. Mine has been a happy, satisfying life. I feel the country has lived up to its promise. Our lives are so much easier now. The only decline is in politics. At my time, politicians were highly educated. Now I don't like the language they use in politics. It has become abusive. In the old days too there were differences, but there was also humanity. They had political differences but personal respect. That is not the case now. Now no one can see eye to eye with people they disagree with.

Our value system was much better. In our times, we lived

in joint families; we lived together and helped each other. Now, that system is no longer there. But you know what, now that I think about it, maybe this is a better system. At that time, one person was earning and feeding seven or eight people. In our family, luckily, there is still a lot of love among brothers and cousins. But not all joint families have that.

Now people focus on earning and educating their children. In our time, we used to retire and then think about constructing a house. Now, people buy homes before they are even forty! We had to wait for our provident fund and gratuity money to build a house. There was no money then. Things are so much better now.

4

Through the Looking Glass

Ganpat Aiyar *is a business projects consultant. He lives in*
Mumbai with his wife, Alexandrina. He was born in 1939.

I was born on 9 September 1939, in Parel, which was the
heart of Bombay. My parents migrated from Kerala to
Bombay, and presumably their parents had migrated from
Tamil Nadu to Kerala. I come from a very politically aware
family. We used to subscribe to some five or six newspapers
including the *Times of India*, *Bombay Chronicle*, *Free Press*
Journal, among others. In fact, one of my earliest memories
is of the floor of our house, strewn with these papers.

Initially, my father worked in a private company; later
he branched out to establish his own business. My mother
was also well educated, although she did not work outside
the house. Both my parents were fluent in English, and they
insisted on speaking to us in it too. I am the middle child; I
had an elder sister and a younger brother. Now it's just me.

We lived in a small apartment, and you know how sound carries far in tiny places. I grew up hearing noisy political discussions. Of course, I was too young to understand what was being said. My father would loudly launch into expositions about the political developments of the day, and my mother would follow with an equally loud, contrarian opinion! This was the background score of my childhood. It used to feel like the strategies of the Second World War emerged from our drawing room. (*Laughs.*)

My father was a stern nationalist, even though you wouldn't think that if you saw him. He had a westernized appearance. He was tall, thin, very handsome with a stentorian voice, and he would liberally quote from Shakespeare. At home, he wore the conventional and traditional dhoti and the sacred thread. Sometimes he would also smear ash on his forehead. But when he stepped out, he was a totally different person. He used to wear double-breasted pinstriped suits or cream coloured suits of thick cotton, tailored by Laffans in Flora Fountain, and polka-dotted Tootal neckties, a quintessential British brand. He was especially partial to the half-Windsor tie knot. On his feet, he wore Oxford Derby brogues, usually tan and sometimes black, polished to a shine. And he finished his look with a soft wool British fedora. This was how he stepped out of the home.

Bombay was largely apolitical then, at least in comparison to Delhi and other places. We were not specifically in the war theatre. Apart from Burma in the east, Ceylon in the south and Afghanistan, the rest of India, by and large, was insulated from the war events that were unfolding. As you travelled further south, the indifference was even more pronounced. Violence in Bombay in those years was largely confined to a few areas. The mill area – where we lived – the Muslim-dominated areas like Bhendi Bazaar and JJ Hospital, and places like that used to see some occasional clashes. By and large, the communities lived in harmony. Sporadic violence, incited by politicians or the British, used to break out. In fact, there were more gang fights than political fights.

One day when I was seven or eight years old I heard that Gandhi was coming to address a meeting at the St Xavier's College ground, which used to be in Parel at the time. This was a bit of a change. Most political meetings used to happen in a place called Gowalia Tank Maidan, which was in central Bombay in Tardeo, near Grant Road.

———————————•———————————

In fact, in 1942 it was at Gowalia Tank that Gandhi announced the Quit India movement.[1] The Maidan was a convenient location, in the heart of the city as well as a few hundred metres down the road from where the Indian National Congress was established. When the Second World War started, Indian nationalists were furious that their country (and the Indian army, which made up the largest forces in the war) had been pulled into the war without any consultation. Two years on, the problems had only worsened. Britain had to deal with both an increasingly serious war situation and a dissatisfied and demoralized Indian army, which was vital to its success. In March 1942, British Prime Minister Churchill sent Sir Stafford Cripps, who was a member of his war cabinet, to India to discuss the country's cooperation in the war in exchange for more rights and devolution of powers. But Cripps was reluctant to offer full independence. Both the Congress and the Muslim League rejected the proposal. Gandhi lost his patience. Maulana Abul Kalam Azad was the president of the All India Congress Committee and organized the meeting at Gowalia Tank. Gandhi declared, 'Here is a mantra, a short one, that I give you. You may imprint it on your hearts and let every breath of yours give expression to it. The mantra is: "Do or Die". We shall either free India or die in the attempt; we shall not live to see the perpetuation of our slavery. Every true Congressman or woman will join the struggle with inflexible determination not to remain alive to see the country in bondage and slavery.'[2]

Anyway, on this particular occasion, he came to Parel. It was a weekend; I was not in school. So, I found my way to the ground by myself and waited to see Gandhi. I couldn't understand a word of what he said because politics was beyond me at that time. But I remember I was thoroughly unimpressed by him. His voice was quite thin; it wasn't the kind of baritone that you paid attention to. In fact, it was rather squeaky. He said something and everyone clapped. So, I did too, and then I walked back home. Later, I had an opportunity to hear Nehru speak. His voice was much better. He had the personality that I thought Gandhi lacked, even though Gandhi gelled more with the population unlike Nehru, who was always seen as some kind of a foreigner.

This meeting was some time after Gandhi had made the call to Quit India (the Bharat Chhodo Andolan). It was the last major civil disobedience movement that occurred before independence. It galvanized the entire population. I read about it in the papers and also overheard my parents talk about it. There were photographs and screaming headlines. I was quite impervious to the details of it, yet I knew something very important was happening. The Quit India movement flagged off a series of violent demonstrations all over the country. Schools were closed, markets were shut. I remember staying home for two or three weeks. Mobs of people went around attacking government property, cutting off telegraph lines and things like that.

It was also the time when a lot of guerrilla warfare techniques were used. People would shoot and scoot. They would tap someone on the shoulder, and when they turned, they would shoot at them and run off. I was witness to some of these incidents myself. We were staying then in a place called Hospital Enclave because all the major hospitals were in that area, including KEM Hospital, Wadia Maternity Hospital, Wadia Children's Hospital, Tata Memorial, etc.

It was a vibrant locality. I remember standing in our

balcony, looking out at some passing parade, and suddenly a fellow appeared from one of the lanes. He came with a knife, stabbed an innocent bystander and ran off. In fact, I have seen this several times. It was shocking.

What was their motivation? It was to simply create a situation of unrest. Later on, it assumed a communal angle; Muslims would kill Hindus and vice versa. At the time, emotions were highly charged. Anything could set people off. I remember another incident. My sister and I were standing in our balcony and watching a Hindu funeral procession go past. Suddenly from the neighbouring building, a woman – or maybe a girl – started giggling. These giggles reached the procession. Immediately, the men from the procession brandished their swords and came running, asking who was laughing. We were terrified. Our parents took us inside and closed the balcony door and told us not to step outside. The police were there, of course.

After a few weeks of all this, though, schools reopened. Even though the riots and violence continued, it was still safe for children on the streets. They wouldn't hurt us. And so, we walked to school and back.

Nationalism was at its peak then. Gandhi had earlier called on all of us to discard Western clothing, and now those demands also grew more vocal. As I mentioned before, my father's entire wardrobe was Western. Without batting an eyelid, my father put all his expensive suits in a bag, and he walked all the way to Gowalia Tank. A big fire was burning there, and my father threw his suits in. He kept two for himself; the rest he burnt. Years later, when he described this incident to me, I could see a glint of regret in his eyes. It had been meaningless, he felt. What was the point that Gandhi was trying to make? It was the bonfire of my father's vanities. Quite literally. Gradually though, he stopped wearing those two suits too. To work, he'd wear regular shirt and trousers. Occasionally, a necktie.

For some time during this period, my uncle used to stay with us. He was twelve years younger than my father, almost like a son to him. In those days, there were posters all over town welcoming the youth to join the armed services. After a small fight, in a moment of anger, my uncle left home and joined the army. For a few years we heard nothing from him. Then one day, we received a picture postcard, the postmark said Melbourne, Australia. He had been captured by the Japanese and was recuperating in a Melbourne hospital after the Allies drove the Japanese away.

Sometime in 1946, there was a knock on the door, and there he was. I was about seven years old at that time. He was dressed in fatigues and army boots and carried a duffle bag. He was a changed man. When he had left, he had been a callow youth, unsure of himself. When he returned, he was a war veteran. He had shrapnel wounds on his right ankle. He had become taciturn and had a faraway look in his eyes.

The wounds of war affect you in more ways than one. He wouldn't talk about what happened to him. I remember he bought a lot of goodies for us – most memorably, he brought tins of condensed milk from Australia. His name was Venkateswaran. But when he came back, he changed it to George V. Waren. And he used to speak with an accent; his habits were Western. He'd become a meat eater. He went on to enjoy a very successful career in the private sector. My father's income was erratic, and whenever we needed financial help, my uncle was always there.

Life sort of plodded on in this manner. Then the independence dates were announced, and there was a tremendous buzz everywhere. All I understood was that the British would go, and we would get our country back. How it would affect our daily lives, I had no idea, obviously. Around that time – in April 1947 – I had to leave my school. It was a girls' school, and boys were allowed only until a certain class. I moved to Don Bosco High School, which meant I had to take the tram to school and back. It was very exciting.

Celebrations started even before Independence Day. Somewhere around 13 August, the government announced that trams would be free so that people could go and see the lighting and celebrations at Victoria Terminus and other parts of the city. We were very excited. On 14 August, we tried to get into a tram, but it was so crowded that we could not even board it. We came back home.

We had a second-hand Marconi radio set at home. On the night of 14 August, we gathered around it and listened to Nehru's speech. 'Long years ago, we made a tryst with destiny, and now the time comes when we shall redeem our pledge, not wholly or in full measure, but very substantially. At the stroke of the midnight hour, when the world sleeps,

India will awake to life and freedom. A moment comes, which comes but rarely in history, when we step out from the old to new, when an age ends, and when the soul of a nation, long suppressed, finds utterance ...'

I remember feeling so proud. The Marconi was a manual tuner. If you touched it, it would jump to another station. I had to keep my hands from fidgeting.

The next day too, we tried to get the tram. Still no luck. Finally, on 16 August, we left home at half-past nine in the night, and we managed to get into a tram. Luckily, we got window seats. What was usually a twenty-minute journey, took an hour that day, but at least we could see the bustle on the streets. We reached Victoria Terminus, and it was stunningly beautiful. Luckily, it didn't rain, and the weather was very pleasant. And the buildings looked so beautiful. I still remember that. We got pushed along with the crowd. We gawked at all the buildings, and we walked all the way to Ballard Pier. I have never seen Bombay so decked up, either before or after that. It was so exciting. There was so much euphoria.

Schools opened on 18 August, which was a Monday. And life went back to normal. Everyone was cheerful. The Italians, who ran my school, were bemused. They didn't really know what was happening. Even our Indian teachers couldn't clearly explain what independence meant. No one quite knew what the future would be like. The school offered us Coca-Cola to celebrate. It was the first time I tasted cola. And it was the first time I ever used a straw. I didn't know what to do. First, I blew into it, and the drink bubbled into my face! It tasted like cough mixture. Delight and disappointment!

The following years were filled with shadows. First was the death of Mahatma Gandhi. Initially, we heard the news through word of mouth. The city felt tense. Suddenly, the shops were closed, and people were running helter-skelter. Everyone thought something would happen. The next morning, we read about it in great detail in the newspapers. That photo of him walking with the women on either side of him is unforgettable. His last march!

Then later that year, there was a devastating cyclone in Bombay. People died; buildings collapsed – the city was paralysed. Soon after, I think, there was a massive earthquake in Assam. I remember seeing these trucks going up and down the street, collecting old clothes and relief materials for the victims. All of these events are mixed up in my head along with the memory of Independence Day.

At the back of my mind I thought if the British had been here they would have handled it better. But at the same time, the other part of me held the British responsible for all these tragic events. I felt that they wanted to prove a point that without them we were nothing.

I remember the American missionaries wanted to fish in troubled waters. Some people from the local Methodist Church came door to door and said this was exactly what the Bible had predicted: the end was near, and this was our only chance to accept Jesus Christ and attain salvation. My mother invited them in and gave them a cup of tea, and also a mouthful! (*Laughs.*)

The other day, I watched a show in which comedian Cyrus Broacha interviewed some young boys and girls about Independence Day, mostly school students and teenagers. Not one person knew the date of Independence. I was shocked. This is so common now. Today's youth have no clue what our history is. They don't know who the chief minister is, who the president is. If this is the state of affairs, I don't know what that means for the future of the country. My children were well aware of what was happening in the political environment. I can't, of course, speak for their children.

When the new dispensation came, I was very excited. I thought this was the leadership we needed when Narendra Modi came to power in 2014. I was tired of the minority appeasement of earlier governments. But things are not going the way I thought; partially because he has more enemies within the country than outside. The media is biased and censored. Consequently, I have stopped reading newspapers. I watch thirty minutes of news television, or when I am on the computer, I take a break and watch some news videos. Even Google gives only negative news.

We have progressed a lot, especially in the last seven or eight years. They have been able to cut through the red tape and come to decisions on issues which were pending for a long time. I like this kind of decisive action. But the quality of our parliamentarians is really poor. The caste system and reservations have been holding the country back. I hope things change soon.

5

Neti, Neti

S. Narendra was born in Mysore in 1940. He worked in the Indian Information Service until he retired.

I was born on 9 May 1940. My family was involved in the fight for freedom from the time of the Quit India movement itself. My father was a lawyer, and he was connected with the Mysore Palace. My mother was illiterate, but she was at the forefront of the freedom movement in our family. I have four siblings. My sister and brother, who are much older than me, had given up their education in response to Gandhiji's call. They were teenagers when I was born.

By the time I was born, my household was deep in the fervour of the independence movement. H.Y. Sharada Prasad, who later became media adviser to Indira Gandhi, used to come to our house, and we used to conduct something known as khadi yagna. During this, we used to spin khadi without a charkha. Instead, we used takli, which was a rudimentary hand spindle used to draw yarn from cotton. The yarn would then be donated for making socks.

Our household was also producing a clandestine newspaper. As a three-year-old, my job was to watch out for the police. Our house was somewhat well known to the authorities, partly because of my father's connection to the palace, but more significantly because a lot of freedom fighters used to hide inside. They used to make me shout, 'Up, up the national flag; down, down the Union Jack.' That was the code that the police were arriving.

On hearing this, whoever was hiding, or making something that they weren't supposed to, would hide the materials and flee. Fortunately, we had a derelict building in the back – they would jump into it and then run away. The police rarely entered the house though, out of respect for my father's association with the royal family. But my father, despite his links to the palace, did not object to any of the family members participating in the freedom movement.

My father's maternal uncle was one of the main administrators of the Mysore Palace estates. An elder brother was an expert veterinarian. The maharaja was a great patron of the turf, and he employed my uncle to look after his horses. The maharaja erected a statue with his name on it when he left the royal service. Despite those connections, my father allowed all these clandestine activities in the household. In fact, he too was donating to the Congress Party. He was also helping some freedom fighters, who were fellow lawyers, when they were imprisoned. He looked after their legal practice and supported their families.

Our home was decorated with photos of our leaders. There were big pictures of Gandhi, Jayaprakash Narayan, J.B. Kripalani, Pandit Nehru, Subhas Chandra Bose and others. They were the icons of those days, like the movie stars of today. Often, during the day, the house was filled with songs. My brother, sister and our friends would practise singing nationalist songs in Kannada.

Supporters of the freedom movement used to organize something called prabhat pheris (early morning processions). People wore the Gandhi cap – men and women – and marched through residential neighbourhoods singing these songs to mobilize public opinion. There weren't many newspapers then, and so, information about what was happening in the movement in other parts of the country was scarce.

The prabhat pheris were used to communicate these things, tell people the freedom movement was vigorously on and to inspire them to continue to fight. Gandhiji had asked his followers to undertake the pheris. Normally these processions were peaceful, and the police wouldn't attack them. These were the sights and sounds of my childhood. I remember them vividly.

I had two uncles, who were much older than my siblings, who used to stay with us. They were my mother's brothers. They would make fake bombs to divert the attention of the police. Mysore was the capital of the princely state, and it had a mighty and strong police force. My uncles would plant these fake bombs to lure the police there, while the freedom fighters could go ahead and do their work elsewhere. Another uncle had a coffee estate. Some freedom fighters who had a price on their heads would be smuggled to the estate in bullock carts, so that they could be safely hidden.

I was too young for most of these activities. I went to school, as usual, in the morning and came back in the afternoon or evening to a house that was in the middle of a revolution. I remember we often had prayer meetings, assemblies, in school. They used to conclude with, 'Oh George Prabhu, protect us,' referring to King George of Britain! After that, we usually sang a state anthem asking Goddess Chamundeshwari to bless the king of Mysore. In those days, often there were meetings in the town hall, which was right in front of the palace. My family was always prominently present in these meetings too. I attended one of the meetings with my mother. I remember the police came and broke it up and asked us to go back home.

In 1947, when India became independent, my state of Mysore took a different path. The maharaja of Mysore, under the influence of a diwan, and along with the rulers of Hyderabad and Travancore, did not want to join the Indian Union. Therefore, we did not celebrate the first Independence Day as it was celebrated in Delhi. In our house, we were all made to get up early in the morning and have a bath. We organized a private ceremony. The national flag was not available. So, my brother made a paper flag, colouring it with crayons, and we hoisted it in our garden. We sang 'Vande Mataram'. As soon as we were done, we removed all evidence of this celebration.

My siblings and mother went for the 'Mysore Challo' demonstration. Their aim was to urge the royal family to join the Indian Union. My elder sisters, one of whom was only thirteen years old, were arrested, and my brother was beaten up quite badly. This agitation to press the maharaja to accede to the Union was intense. My sisters and mother and older cousins also used to picket government offices, schools and colleges as part of the movement.

That year, the diwan of Travancore, C.P. Ramaswami Iyer, was brutally attacked, and the angry mob almost cut off his nose. That was when the maharaja of Travancore, Chithira Thirunal, relented. On hearing this, the diwan of Mysore – Ramasamy Mudaliar, twin brother of the famous educationist and doctor Lakshmanasamy Mudaliar – developed cold feet and ran away to Madras overnight. Then the maharaja of Mysore also agreed to join the Indian Union.

———————•———————

The maharaja of Mysore, Jayachamaraja Wadiyar, had signed the Instrument of Accession in early August 1947.[1] However, no one was clear what the future course of action would be. The Congress unit in the state, which had set up Praja Paksha – a people's party – had as its primary aim the idea of establishing a 'responsible government'. K.C. Reddy, the founder of Praja Paksha, was the man who called for the 'Mysore Challo' movement. It was a satyagraha, on Gandhiji's lines, and their demand was that a royal proclamation of the formation of a democratically accountable government be made. They also demanded the formation of an interim ministry and a constitution committee of twenty-five people to draft a state constitution. All political prisoners were also to be released. In front of a crowd of nearly fifty thousand people, Reddy raised the flag of the Indian Union. He declared that until a responsible government was appointed, they would not fly the Mysore state flag.

The marches in support of the 'Mysore Challo' movement intensified over the next few weeks.[2] In early September, Reddy, other leaders and scores of protesters were arrested by the police. Those in jail were subjected to violent treatment by the police. News of the arrests and police brutality further enraged the protesters, and more people joined their numbers. In the ensuing chaos of the protests, in one incident, the police fired to control the crowd, and a college student lost his life. On another day, a swarm of protesters attempted to enter the palace. This time too, police firing killed a man. A two-day curfew was imposed, but the protesters mostly defied it. More than twenty people eventually died in this agitation. The deadline for the princely states to join the Union was 14 September. In the run-up to the date, the protests further intensified. Crowds of people marched the streets, picketed courts, colleges and government buildings, and barricaded all the main roads. They waved the national flag everywhere.

Then the police turned, and they too joined the movement. Around the same time, the workers in the gold mines also went on strike and stopped work. The continued intensity of the protests, and the lack of a police force to effectively quell it, eventually left the maharaja with no choice other than to accede to the Union of India and set up a democratic government.

My childhood was shaped by the freedom movement. My mother would tell me stories about Gandhiji and other leaders. We thought our leaders were our heroes and developed a hatred for foreign rule. The news of the Partition – the massacres and the rapes – and photographs of these atrocities, circulating in Mysore, heightened these emotions. This is what shaped our early impressions about India and, in fact, this in a way persuaded me to join the civil service.

Once we got independence, we thought better people would lead us, and we would conquer the problems of poverty and inequality. Our own household was not well off. There were hardly any grains because of rationing. Food was scarce. Money was scarce. But we thought once independence came, things would improve. We did not have much of an idea of what that improvement was supposed to be. (*Laughs*.) But, at least, we thought there would be more food to eat.

My brother and sister lost precious years in the movement. Because of that, their education was delayed. And there were no jobs to be had. It was, once again, the same hard life. My own life didn't change much, though now there was hardly any income. My father had given up much of his practice because of various circumstances. Besides, most of the cases he took up were on behalf of the poor. They couldn't afford to pay him. We struggled, and whatever little money we had also could not buy anything because of rationing and shortages. There was a thriving black market for everything. I don't think India changed much once independence was declared.

In 1948, something happened that I will never forget. We used to play football in various parks of Mysore. We could not afford a football in those days, so we would play with a tennis ball. Next to the park, we used to see some people come in khaki knickers around five in the evening. Often, they finished their meeting and then hung around us, watching us play. Sometimes, they used to tell us stories. As small boys, of course we used to listen to them.

One day, they distributed laddoos to us. When we asked what the occasion was, the man said, 'A dog called Gandhi would be dead.' I went home and told my mother what I had heard. She started beating me. In Kannada, if you say something bad, you repent it by saying 'bidthu, bidthu, bidthu' (give it up, give it up, give it up). The next day, again I got beaten up because Gandhiji was actually assassinated! My brother heard the news on the radio, and he raced home and told my mother. My mother yelled at me saying I had brought the bad news one day earlier. My house was engulfed in grief by the news. Yes, Nehru was my hero, but Gandhi was a saint.

By this time, the first feelings of disenchantment had set in. Mysore state was better ruled than most. Yet, in the years just after independence there was a feeling that the rule of the maharaja was better than that of the local politicians. Corruption started; casteism intensified. The real freedom fighters did not get a chance to run the country. The power brokers took over. My parents and siblings used to discuss this and often expressed their frustration with these new politicians and the moneyed people. They felt a sense of loss. This was not what they had dreamt of. They felt betrayed. The hope was that the country would be run by people like Sardar Patel or J.P. Narayan who worked honestly for the good of the many rather than to enrich a few.

Within a decade, politics in the state really started disintegrating. Delhi, I am sure, was no different, but seen from a distance of over twenty-five hundred kilometres from Mysore, it seemed better. Nehru was still there; there were some freedom fighters who were still ministers. They had certain ideals.

By then, even my nationalist parents and siblings started to think that perhaps we had been better off under the maharaja. Of course, once the Chinese aggression started in 1962, a new patriotic fervour took over the country. Wars always do that. After the independence struggle, my sister and brother resumed their education. My sister became a teacher. My brother became a civil engineer and also took up teaching. They are not alive any more.

In Mysore, we had very little information about what was going on in the country. Whatever we heard was a diluted version. My family were avid consumers of news, so we were slightly better informed. Once I grew up and started reading for myself, I got a better understanding of what really was happening in the country. I read about the Planning Commission, the infrastructure push, the big dams being built and new educational institutions being set up. Nehru was our hero, and we thought as long as Nehru was there, our future was safe.

But all of us had the same regrets that the idealism of our youth, the values of Gandhiji, had all been wiped off. One of the great things of those days was that poverty was such that there wasn't much class differentiation. You were either rich or poor; there wasn't a significant middle class (but caste differentiation existed, of course). There wasn't a robust middle class – it was only a robust poor class.

After school, I joined the government college because we could not afford professional colleges. I took humanities and did my master's from the University of Mysore. After that, I took the civil service exam. There was idealism on my part. I thought I could do a lot more for the country as a civil servant than if I worked in the private sector.

For a while, before I got through the services, I worked for the State Bank of India. There was no job satisfaction at all.

Banking, especially before nationalization, had very little to do with helping the people who needed it. I was relieved to resign from the bank and join the services, even though my pay was much lower. I have no regrets about this.

Unfortunately, the day I got my results for the civil service exam was the day Nehru died (27 May 1964). It was bittersweet. I was excited for myself but bereaved at the news and what it meant for the country. Nehru had been the lifeline of our country. What would we do without him?

I joined the Indian Information Service. I was posted all over, from Patna to all over Karnataka, and then I moved to Delhi, worked in various ministries and eventually retired as adviser to the prime minister. I had a fantastic experience working in the government. I worked with Indira Gandhi, Y.B. Chavan, Morarji Desai, P.V. Narasimha Rao, Chandra Shekhar, I.K. Gujral, Deve Gowda and A.B. Vajpayee. In the bank, I would not have had any such exposure or experience.

Nehru may have gone, but we still had stalwarts when I started working for the government. I experienced my first Parliament session in 1966–67. The debates used to be so interesting, and party members themselves used to criticize the government. It was such a terrific atmosphere. I have seen the liveliest of parliament sessions in 1966–67, where the prime minister was not spared, and no minister was spared. Parliamentarians could carry independent views, and the government used to listen to them. Today, public opinion does not matter. Respect for institutions has gone away.

I do think about the way that Nehru's legacy is being

distorted now. There is a great book by Diana L. Eck called *India: A Sacred Geography*. There, she says how the Muslim invaders who came to India wanted to destroy the icons of Hinduism because as long as the icons were there, they could not shine. Today's story is similar. The previous icons must be destroyed to make oneself great.

On Indira Gandhi's hundredth birth anniversary, nobody wrote about her, but I did. All leaders have a mixed legacy. I have seen power from close quarters. Most leaders were visionaries, and they gave something to the country. Y.B. Chavan was a great leader. Morarji Desai had his faults, his personal likes and dislikes, but he was a man of steel. Indira Gandhi – what a mixed legacy – but her budget in 1970 was a seminal budget. It looked for the first time at inequality, poverty, etc. Narasimha Rao always had empathy for the poor. Inequality was something that kept all of them awake. Today, not a single state or centre politician cares about inequities, social or economic. It is very different now.

In the early days after independence, some extreme measures had to be taken. Nationalization of banks and insurance were both necessary steps. They were all being misused thoroughly by a few who were rich and powerful. Indian agriculture hardly got any credit. Those days, public sector institutions did a lot of good work; they had extraordinary vision. But then they were misused. They were destroyed. Today, the idea is to first make them worthless and then sell them.

People are totally lost. Once economic reforms were

introduced, there was some idealism. It was clear that the previous model had not worked. But today, economic reforms are not to benefit the public or for the larger good, it is only about how much money individuals can make. The entire political establishment is engaged in economic reforms to benefit themselves, and industry is playing along. One is sad that inequality is rising and is so visible all around us. At one time, ostentatious consumption was frowned upon; today it is celebrated. I am shocked that even liquor and pan masala advertisements reign supreme now.

My parents were around for a significant period in post-independence India. My father passed away in 1980 and my mother, in 1990. Coming from old Mysore, especially people who have lived through the reign of Krishna Raja Wadiyar (that is, until 1940), they certainly had their regrets. Krishna Raja Wadiyar was a visionary who did many good things, even though he was constrained by the British. He sold off his family heirloom to set up an irrigation tank at the confluence of river Kaveri and its tributaries. Can you think of anyone today who will do something like this?

Of course, there is an argument that people's lives have become better in the last seventy-five years. But what is the number of people whose lives haven't? As the middle class has grown, we have begun to forget about the poor. Yes, some have prospered, but others' lives have deteriorated. You can see both sides of this story. 'Neti, Neti', as they say in Indian philosophy.

6

The Nation Builders

Sarabjit A. Singh *was born in Lahore in September 1943. He worked in Indian Railways and retired as a general manager. He was a member of the Principal Bench of the Central Administrative Tribunal. He also worked with the World Bank on disability issues and is a frequent contributor to various English newspapers.*

I was born in Lahore in September 1943. My father was an officer in the agriculture department. I lived with my parents. I have two sisters. One was born in 1947 and the other in 1950. My grandparents were in the village at the time, which was luckily on this side of the border.

I remember we lived in a biggish sort of house in Lahore. At least for me as a child, it appeared big. It was on 5, Bahawalpur Road. I once asked a friend who was going to Pakistan if he could locate it. He could find 4 and 6, but he could not locate 5. He said there were some shops that were constructed in front of it. But all I remember is that it was a biggish house with a large garden. There was a gurdwara in the back.

In the lead-up to Partition, I have vague memories about the conversations around me. I certainly had the sense that life was disturbed. Master Tara Singh was the leader of the Sikhs at the time. He had given a call that we should protest against the partition and sleep on the ground. I remember we did that for a time in our home. I was only four years old, but I knew that things were not normal and that they were beginning to change.

Since my father was in the government, we were one of the few people in the area who had a car and a driver. Those days, during and right after the war, petrol was rationed. My father would get coupons for buying petrol. He began saving them. He would walk to office, in fact, to save petrol.

During this time, mid-1947, independence was announced and Partition was being discussed. In a few weeks, my father started hearing that maybe it was time to start moving. Things around us were beginning to get worse, and riots were taking place. First, we shifted from Bahawalpur and went to a suburb of Lahore called Krishna Nagar, which was a Hindu-dominated area. But in a few days, it was clear that we were not safe there either.

There was no choice but to leave Lahore. We got into the car with whatever we could carry in it, locked up the house and left. We started driving. The distance between Lahore and Amritsar is only fifty kilometres, but the road was full of people. They were walking right in the middle, and they wouldn't give way to the car. We ended up taking a longer route via Ferozepur.

I still remember seeing people walking with small bundles of their possessions on their heads. My father then met a police officer whom he knew, and he took us safely across to the Indian side. We came to Jalandhar. Our driver's name was Kulwant Singh. His family was living elsewhere, in a village close to the new border. He went back there after dropping us and realized that his whole family had been murdered. Only his son, who had pretended to be dead, had survived the massacre. It was traumatic. Everyone we knew had lost someone or the other.

After the lavish house in Lahore, we were now living in a small room in Jalandhar. Strangely, the one thing I clearly remember is that we used to get eggs in tins. Powdered eggs! It was the American food ration. You reconstituted the powder and made eggs. But generally, all around us, things were not safe. My father left us in our ancestral village near Ludhiana. My mother and I stayed there with my grandparents, uncles, aunts and cousins.

In the meantime, my father went to look for where his new office, the Department of Agriculture, was to be established. The thing is, no one had really thought through these things. Everything happened in such a rush. There was fear everywhere. Not only were there people attacking others, but vandalism and looting too had started.

As the Muslims were being driven off, gangs of people started looting the better off non-Muslim families too. We were worried that we would be attacked and robbed. I remember my uncles and cousins would climb on the roof of the house, and they would carry their guns and keep watch from there. And I remember my paternal grandmother, who was a very old woman at the time, would get hysterical. It was a fraught time.

My father found out that his office would be in Dagshai, a place near Kasauli. Eventually, after a few weeks, we moved there. On 15 August, we were in Dagshai. There was no celebration. There was no joy. There was only misery and trauma. We had a staff member. He came into the house and announced, 'Oh-ji, the English have gone.' And that's how I became aware of the fact.

There was a Gorkha troop in the cantonment next to where we lived. They played a football match to mark the occasion the next day, I think. But as far as I remember, there was no joy that we had become independent. Our lives had been shattered.

People who came from the Pakistan side had to be rehabilitated. They had to declare themselves as refugees. Our thought was that our land was not on that side; we were originally from Ludhiana and we only owned the house in Lahore. We had seen the kind of looting that was happening in houses that were occupied, so you can imagine what houses that were abandoned were like. There was no way that we would get anything back. Going to Lahore was an impossibility. My mother had no hope of ever getting back any of the possessions she had left behind.

Soon, we moved from Dagshai to Simla, where the Department of Agriculture was established. I started going to school in Simla. In fact, I went to a girls' school; they allowed boys only in kindergarten. We were there till 1952. I learned to ice skate, I remember. Simla was a fun place for a kid.

There was something called PEPSU then – the Patiala and East Punjab States Union. All the princely states in that region were combined together into one state called PEPSU. There was a huge law and order problem in that region, and Naxalism was rampant. It was, in fact, the first state in India where President's Rule was established. The maharaja, Yadavindra Singh, was a very tall and handsome man. He was quite impressive. He acted as the raj pramukh (constitutional head of a state formed from several princely states). When President's Rule was imposed, my father was asked to go there, along with the administrator, and help get their agriculture going. My family moved to Nabha, which is near Patiala.

My childhood in Nabha too was very interesting. I was nine years old when we moved. We were the privileged lot. We could do no wrong. Feudalism ensured that the ruling class could get away with anything. We had vehicles with red number plates. The red plates indicated that the vehicle was a palace property. Our jeep was Patiala 56! I learned to drive in it. Nobody would question you if you were in a red number plate car.

We would get up early in the morning, at 4 a.m., and go for shikar. My father didn't go, but his friends did. I was given a .410 – a small-bore shotgun. We shot partridges mostly, and some other birds. These were then cooked and eaten. In the evenings, sometimes we would go for another round. We lived in the cantonment and used to have massive barbecues in the evening. As kids, we could move around the area quite freely. If you made friends with the tank drivers, they would even take you for a ride in them.

Even as I was enjoying my youth, people around us were beginning to rebuild their broken lives. Since my father was in the government, the disruption in our family was minimal, in a way, as compared to many others. My father's job remained and, in fact, because the British had left, a large number of opportunities opened up for people like him.

My father was just the right age for a new country. He had studied in Lyallpur, which today is known as Faisalabad. He topped the university. In fact, I still have his gold medal. After that, he completed his PhD from the UK in 1937. How many people went to study abroad at that time? So, he was much sought after as an agricultural economist. Life, at least for my family, improved after the British left. In his career, my father reached levels he perhaps couldn't have had the British been there. He was in his forties when he became the director of agriculture of Punjab, which at that time included Haryana and Himachal Pradesh. My father established the Board for Economic Enquiry. He wrote the chapters on farm accounting in the *Handbook of Indian Agricultural Research*.

Today when we are sitting on a mountain of food grains, it is hard to imagine that in the 1950s India did not grow enough food to feed its growing population and depended on supplies shipped from the US. We lived, as it was said, from ship to mouth. What changed all that was the green revolution. My father, along with other experts, authored the ground breaking report – 'India's Food Crisis and Steps to Meet It'. It laid out the road map for India's food security. The interesting thing was that my parents, and lots of other people we know, never thought badly of Muslims. There was no rancour. There was acceptance that both sides did terrible things, and they laid the blame on the leaders. Nehru, Gandhi and Jinnah were not popular in Punjab. Punjabis felt that Partition was thrust upon them. They hadn't wanted it, and yet they had to suffer the consequences. They were clear that these leaders brought it upon us, and that they had unleashed the beast within, which resulted in the massacres and deaths.

Since Nabha lacked quality schooling, I was sent to boarding school – Lawrence School, Sanawar. It was a very British school, of course. I am now aware of my privilege. But at the time, I was oblivious to it. Most of the other students came from landed families in Punjab. The remaining were from the armed forces and services. We were all from a certain socio-economic class. I grew up in a rarefied atmosphere. We were young people occupying a place of privilege in a country that was at the cusp of a new beginning.

Punjab was being rebuilt. Chandigarh was being built.

There was huge excitement that things were happening. In Chandigarh homes, conversations were always around Corbusier. It was a great atmosphere. We felt we were going to do great things.

After finishing school, I went to Government College, Chandigarh. That time, the only focus was on getting a good job. Those days our options were either to get into the civil service, join the army, or maybe become a professor. A few people joined British companies in Calcutta or went abroad. I wanted to be a mechanical engineer, it was the best choice then. The sense was that the country was going to build infrastructure, and mechanical engineers would be at the forefront of building a new India.

Indian Railways had a scheme called the Special Class Railway Apprentice for training mechanical and electrical engineers. After passing 10+2, one could take the entrance examination by the UPSC and get into the Indian Railways Institute of Mechanical and Electrical Engineering, which was popularly known by the name of Jamalpur, the place where it is located in Bihar. They took only about ten to fifteen people a year. It was an extremely tough competition. Some fifty thousand people appeared in my year and ten of us got in.

You studied in the institute, they paid you a stipend, and you were going to be the elite in the railways. Getting into it itself was a big thing. I was ranked second in the UPSC examination. I joined the institute. The moment one started there, they were in the heart of the nation-building process.

In the institute, I started getting the feeling that we had made it and we were the best of the best, and our job was to build the country.

On starting work, our salaries were not great, of course. In fact, some of my batchmates later went to the US. But I didn't go; I wrote in my diary – where I argued with myself – about whether I should go to the US and join Harvard or Stanford University, or stay here. I came to the conclusion that I would rather be here and build the country than go and be a part of the American middle class in the US, where one would always be below a WASP.

I'd rather take my chances here, and see where I could go. I have never regretted that choice. I am better off in so many ways than my batchmates who went abroad. They may have a little more money than me, but theirs is a lonely life. People tend to get estranged. In the beginning you feel darn good, but then the satisfaction starts dipping. I have no regrets – the railways gave me a lot. I have lived a good life.

My specific contribution, when I was in the Railways Design and Standards Organization, was to develop individual projects by reverse engineering. One of my projects was to create an indigenous lubricating oil for diesel locomotives. It may seem simple, but it's not. It was a complex process, and it required an additive package, which was a closely guarded secret.

So, the Government of India set up a team with members from the railway, defence and petroleum ministries, among others, to come up with solutions, evaluate the quality of these solutions and see if they fit the requirements. It was an exciting time. I was the person who cleared the first indigenous lubricating crankcase oil called Servo 402. Other steel plants and mammoth organizations like BHEL, massive fertilizer plants, were all coming up around the same time. There was great enthusiasm. We absolutely felt like we were building a new country.

In the mid-1980s, I found myself having to pay a big price because of another freedom movement of sorts. I had just come back from Mozambique, where I had gone on deputation to assist in maintaining their diesel locomotives. When I returned to India, I was posted to South Eastern Railway in Visakhapatnam. I was quite happy there.

Militancy was rampant in Punjab during this time, and Rajiv Gandhi, who was prime minister then, announced that he was setting up a railway coach factory in the state. They started calling people to come and join that pilot team. I was asked and so I decided to go. My parents lived close by, in Chandigarh, and I belonged to that part of the country. This was in 1986.

It was a great posting. It was a challenge in those circumstances to build one of the largest coach manufacturing plants in the whole world. And we had to do it in two years.

My job was to recruit and train three thousand people in two years. It was a great assignment. And, it was a great achievement!

A few months into the project, I discovered some people had committed fraud. I confronted them and they felt that

I would not be intimidated easily. So, they got hold of some local terrorists in the village who tried to kill me and my wife. The times were bad; so many people I knew had been shot. My neighbour, who was a sessions judge, was shot at. The DIG of Punjab Police, Julio Ribeiro, was shot at in the police headquarters! His security officer, who I had met six days before, was killed in that attack.

This is how it happened. One evening, my wife and I went for a walk in the railway colony. We went to an area which, in retrospect, we should have avoided because it was deserted. Some guys came on a scooter and stopped in front of us. One of them got down, took out a pistol, and before I knew it, he had pumped a bullet into me. It was all so fast, I didn't know what happened. I was frozen and couldn't run. My wife too was in shock. We were looking at each other, unable to move. And then he shot again. The second bullet injured my spine, and I fell.

He then shot my wife. The bullet went next to her ear and lodged in her jaw. Then he came back to me, I was still on the ground, and he shot me again. This bullet went between my heart and my lung. Then he put the pistol to my head and pulled the trigger. But the shot didn't fire. I remember it clearly. I could see the sparks from the percussion cap from the corner of my eyes as the revolver was fired but nothing happened. He had no more bullets left, and they went away.

My wife, who was injured and bleeding, ran and got help. Railways, luckily, is a well-trained organization. They know how to handle emergencies. Everyone came running

to help us. They divided themselves into groups. Some
went to look after our daughters; other went to get a doctor
and an ambulance, etc. The funny part is that I was setting
up the hospital in the campus and had just purchased
two ambulances. One of these ambulances came for me
and the other for my wife. We were the first ones to use
them. (*Laughs.*)

I was taken to the Civil Hospital in Kapurthala, where they
stabilized me. I was one of the senior officers on the campus,
so this incident came as a big shock to the community. The
deputy commissioner came immediately to the hospital, in
his pyjamas, in fact. Then, I was shifted to CMC Hospital
in Ludhiana. The whole administration showed up for me.

Before this incident, I used to meet the governor of
Punjab, Sidharth Shankar Ray, each month and brief him
on the progress of the factory. So, he knew who I was and
he came to meet me and took up my case very strongly. The
Punjab Police caught my assailants in ten days. Madhavrao
Scindia was the railway minister. He rang me up from
Australia and wrote a letter to me. I still have it. He also
wrote to my father. The maharaja of Kapurthala came.
I got a hell of a lot of help. Then I was sent to England
for rehabilitation and further treatment. But I have been
confined to a wheelchair since. I have never walked again.

I think back to that day very often. I made a fundamental
mistake. When you are in an institution like the railways,
you always have some issues or the other going on with
unions and things like that. As long as you are fair, things

get resolved. I did not realize that because of militancy, the conditions in Punjab were different. I should not have treated the tensions around me like it was part of everyday life.

Previously, I had worked in Uttar Pradesh and had taken things like this in my stride. I regret not taking this dispute more seriously here. It changed the way I wanted to live my life. It made me not take the kind of risks I would have taken otherwise. I was certain I had a great future outside the Railways too, but that was closed to me now. I had to stay within the arms of the Railways because they had been supportive of my difficulties. They took care of me. I don't know if a private sector company would have done that.

Before I was shot, I was certain that I would shift from the Railway Board to a ministry and from there to an organization like the UN. That was what I wanted to do, but it was not to be. Working with agencies like the World Bank (for which I did some work post my retirement) and the IMF would have involved a lot of international travel, and that was a constraint for me. My wife would have had to come along with me everywhere. There is no point brooding over things now. Unpleasant things happen, and you have to take it in your stride.

I am very disturbed by what is happening in the country now. This is not the country we were trying to build when we were young. I started service in the 1960s. Nehru's time overlapped my life by seventeen years. I had seen Nehru when I was a kid, and he was a charismatic and outstanding guy. There is no doubt about that. He was a patriot and a democrat.

The 'Nehruvian Consensus' was something we all believed in. Whatever people may say now, at our time, we all believed in it. The value system which he put forward – self-sufficiency, a socialistic pattern of society, democracy and secularism – these were the underlying principles on which we worked. My job, and my contemporaries' jobs, was to build that base for this country. By being part of the process of industrialization in the country, I felt I had helped in building the nation.

———————●———————

Nehru created a system of governance that sought to take the middle path, eschewing the extremism of the left and the right. The key pillars of his vision for a New India were multiparty democracy on the Westminster model; equality of all citizens regardless of gender, class and religion; a mixed economy, with the government playing a 'commanding role' in promoting industrial development; a foreign policy based on non-alignment with the superpowers of the day, the US and the Soviet Union. The expression 'Nehruvian Consensus' was subsequently coined to illustrate these ideals. In a paper titled 'Rise and Demise of Nehruvian Consensus: A Historical Review', Chanchal Kumar Sharma writes, 'The English speaking "progressive" elite demonstrated a natural affinity for centralized government control as a means to achieve Nehruvian goals of social justice, secularism, and economic growth. The "steel frame" of the "enlightened technocratic bureaucracy" became, by default, a vehicle for the "activist state".[1]

A popular cartoon by R.K. Laxman illustrates the trouble with this model. In it, Nehru is shown trying to play a sitar, a trumpet and a horn. On his feet are two cymbals. Surrounding him is a whole bunch of party men. A tabla lies to one side. The speech blurb has Nehru saying, 'Is there a tabla player in the audience? No? Very well ...' as he turns to play that too.

———————•———————

But, around the late 1970s, the 'Nehruvian Consensus' was giving way. In Mozambique, I once attended a party where the Indian ambassador was present. And I think the British ambassador came and asked, 'What do you think is the biggest problem of India today?' I blurted out, speaking out of turn, of course (*laughs*), that we needed to create a new consensus, because we had lost what held us together in the previous couple of decades.

We knew, at the time, that the consensus had gone, perhaps it was outdated, and it wasn't working well. That was maybe the time we should have changed like China did. Unfortunately, Indira Gandhi tried to create a weakish form of a 'Nehruvian Consensus', when the pillars of 'self-sufficiency' and 'commanding heights of the economy' were already showing signs that they weren't working. That's what caused most problems. Then, when they eventually dismantled the Inspector Raj, it was twenty years too late. It should have been done in the 1970s. The signs were all there.

Overall, I think the country has delivered on some promises but failed on others. When we were growing up, India was in the process of being created. We didn't think in terms of being Indian, people thought of themselves as Punjabis or Bengalis or whatever. The concept of Indian was new; it barely existed. India that way was an artificial country. The states had to be united. The constitution had to be written. Administrative procedures had to be set up. There was no middle class. It was either top or bottom.

But a lot of work was done. The Indian Institutes of Management were set up; ISRO came up. Look at Chandigarh. I saw the city being built before my eyes. There was amazing dynamism. Nehru himself supervised many of these infrastructure projects, especially the dams. He called them the 'temples of new India'. He was so open.

The Punjab High Court is a beautiful building. Corbusier designed the parking in the basement, and no one was allowed to park in front. But the judges began doing so, which led to oil dripping from their cars, staining the entrance, and other problems. Corbusier is said to have taken a photo of that and written to Nehru, saying, 'Look at what your judges are doing to my buildings.' And Nehru, of course, settled it so that nobody ever dared park their cars in front of the building.

The chief minister of Punjab at that time was Pratap Singh Kairon, an extremely dynamic guy, who was part of the Ghadar Movement and was educated in California. Harvey Slocum was the man who built the Bhakra Nangal Dam. When he found something was wrong, he would scribble his concerns on a piece of paper and send it to Kairon. And that was it. Whatever concerns he had were immediately addressed and resolved. There was a 'get things done' mentality then. It was an amazing time.

The biggest failure of India is that democracy has been imposed from the top. Now I feel that education and healthcare for the people at the bottom was not given the importance it deserved. It was too elitist, and we are paying the price for it.

I don't know what's going to happen and whether we will ever go back to our secular values. All I know is what I learned from Punjab, that is if you ride a tiger, it's impossible to dismount it. If you start stoking polarization and hatred, you are asking for trouble. In Punjab in the 1980s, the difference was that the polarization they tried to create between Hindus and Sikhs was not there in reality. So, it was forced and, therefore, didn't endure.

Till very recently, I was very happy to be a part of the country. I felt most proud to be an Indian when I was in Mozambique, where my main job was to show that we were no less than the white man. And we proved it. It was the height of the Cold War, and Mozambique was a front line state.

In the last few years, I have begun to feel despondent about the country. Things were going all right until Manmohan Singh's time. Maybe we could have done more, but we were largely all right. There was a sense that we were on the right track. But now, there is despondency; not only with me, many of my friends too feel the same way. But what do we do? The reality is that in the 1970s the Chinese were worse than us. And today look at where they are. That is the disappointment. It's not that we don't have the capability. But we just can't seem to get our act together.

In a way, it is the sign of the success of a democracy. Giving everybody a vote has meant that it has got people who were out of the system into positions of decision-making. But they don't have the background of information and knowledge to see how the system runs. I was talking to a friend of mine the other day about the results of the recent state elections in Punjab. I said, 'The person who defeated the chief minister, Charanjit Singh Channi, was someone from a village who repaired mobile phones for a living. There is a total change in the social class of people who are in power. We don't know anyone in the new regimes.'

My friend said, 'The argument is that if you put yourself in that person's shoes, you will come to know what the problems of India really are.' And my answer was, 'Yes, I have to put myself in his shoes to understand what the problems of India are. But then he has to put himself in my shoes to understand what the solutions could be.'

My experience has been that when such people come,

they think they can do anything. They don't understand they have to work within the constitutional provisions. A friend of mine, who is an IAS officer, said a new chief minister came and told him to 'arrest this guy'. My friend said that you can't just arrest someone like that, and there has to be a charge, and an FIR and things like that.

The chief minister was aghast. He said, 'If a police officer can arrest anybody, why can't I?' Now, this is the attitude all the way up to the highest offices in the country. The Westminster system has basically changed to a presidential system, but without its checks and balances. That's a tragedy. I don't know where this is going to end.

7

Hijinks in Hazratganj

Saeed Naqvi is a senior journalist and commentator who has written for prominent Indian and international publications. He is also the author of several books, the latest of which, The Muslim Vanishes, was published in 2022.

What is my date of birth? (*Long pause.*) It was so long ago, let me think. Ah, I was born on 24 May 1941 in Mustafabad, Uttar Pradesh. In the old days, my ancestors had some land. But when the lands began to go, they did not want to serve anybody, and so they went into independent professions.

The profession that was easiest for them was law. Most of them became lawyers, some teachers. My father was also a lawyer. He practised in Lucknow. My mother was mostly self-taught. Girls used to be taught at home, and my mother learned Arabic, Farsi and Urdu. They all knew a smattering of Sanskrit too.

Awadhi and Braj Bhasha were, of course, very much a

part of my family home in Mustafabad. Our house was not a palace; it was not a grand building. But it was a haveli, where all my family members gathered for Eid, Bakr Eid and other festive occasions. Muharram was very important because we are Shias. In fact, the family get-together on Muharram was so important that once when my maternal uncle said he couldn't come because he had his examinations, he was told, 'These are just your BA exams, you can always write them later. Come home for Muharram.'

As you can see, these were feudal people. They were educated at home. The formal education in schools and colleges came a little later. They were all proud of their Urdu culture, and the language played a big role in Partition. People don't realize it because Hindi and Khari Boli were posed as counterparts to Urdu. But in and around Lucknow, people were very proud of their Urdu in speech, songs and poetry. And so, they wouldn't learn English. They really believed that Hindus and Muslims had fought the British together, which indeed they had.

In 1857, my own ancestor, Mir Baqar, was arrested for helping Rana Beni Madhav, who led a rebellion against the British. Beni Madhav is very famous, there is a hospital in his name in Raebareli. Rana Beni Madhav escaped to Nepal, but Mir Baqar was arrested. He and twelve of his accomplices were hanged and, as was the old custom of the British, their bodies were left hanging on a tamarind tree outside the collectorate as a deterrent for others.

Mir Baqar's son, therefore, was thrown into penury and

had to go begging. Now remember, the police and everybody who had hanged Mir Baqar were all Indians. When Indians began to serve the British, they were very hard on their own people. Mir Baqar's son, Mir Waheed, could only go and visit a few relatives at night, under cover of darkness. Of course, the relatives were also very cautious because being seen with him would bring them trouble.

Anyway, Mir Waheed's son Mir Wajid Ali – I know this sounds like a Dickens novel – studied at the Raebareli railway station under a street lamp. He became a very distinguished lawyer, and he and Motilal Nehru became good friends and that friendship was further consolidated when they were together in Maini Jail. They had a professional and personal liking for each other. Mir Wajid Ali was my father's grandfather. My grandfather too was a lawyer, as was my father. My sister is the fourth-generation lawyer in the family. And now my granddaughter is studying law and she will be the fifth.

There are seven of us siblings. I am the eldest. The family was divided in two. The ones who were more educated came from my mother's side. My mother was from a distinguished family of Barabanki. Since they were educated, they were all communists. (*Laughs.*) My maternal uncle had the greatest influence on me, intellectually. He, along with Kaifi Azmi, Majrooh Sultanpuri, Sajjad Zaheer and others, were carted off to the Bombay communes by the very colourful CPI Secretary General P.C. Joshi.

That was when the Progressive Writers' Movement

came into being. So, my family's affiliation with cinema
and literature is irrevocably interlinked with all this. Kaifi
Azmi used to often come and stay with us in our house in
Lucknow. I would say my uncle and his friends groomed
Azmi into Marxism and the Progressive Movement.

Let me tell you a funny story. When the now famous
actress Shabana was put into a convent school in Bombay,
they wanted to interview the parents. Kaifi couldn't speak a
word of English, nor could his wife, Shaukat. So, a common
friend of my uncle and Kaifi's, called Munish Narain Saxena,
escorted young Shabana and pretended to be her father. In
those days, there was no television or social media, so no one
knew what Kaifi looked like. And that is how Shabana Azmi
became an English-speaking girl!

So, back to my life. The family was divided into two: one
was the Marxist side, and the other, the Mir Wajid Ali side,
were Congressis closely associated with the Nehrus. In fact,
Motilal used to come home and say, 'Hamare liya khana, aur
Jawahar ke liye bhojan' (Food for me, and vegetarian food
for Jawahar).

Panditji had come under the spell of Gandhiji and
because he had to work among the people, he had cut a
little bit of non-vegetarian food out of his diet. Motilal was
a colourful man. Toh aise taluqaat the (The relationship was
such). 'To jab aise taluqaat the' that Panditji (We could not
call him Jawaharlal. My grandfather would yell at us across
the hallway if he heard us say Jawaharlal. We had to call
him Panditji or Pandit Nehru.) was a prominent figure in
our lives.

Gandhi was not so high in their esteem because, according to one of my grandparents, there was some doubt about his sartorial eccentricities. Nehru wore an achkan, he placed a rose in his lapel, and he spoke chaste Urdu. Nehru was a Kashmiri Pandit, and Kashmiri Pandits made significant contributions to Urdu right from the Awadh era. There are two distinct kinds of Kashmiri Pandits – those in the Valley, and those that came down to Awadh and they, in fact, dominated Urdu literature. They spoke better Urdu than the Muslims. A great prose writer in Urdu was Pandit Ratan Nath Sarshar who was a Kashmiri Brahmin. In my village, during Muharram, Pandit Pran Nath Kacher used to come to deliver the sermons on the tragedy of Karbala.

It was a very integrated culture, intellectually. As I have said a million times, my mother's and my grandmother's favourite sohar (a song sung on the birth of a child) was 'Allah miyan, humre bhaiyya kar diyo Nandlal' (Oh Allah, give my brother a son like Lord Krishna). Another story was that of Fatima Bibi, the Prophet's daughter. While waiting for her husband, Hazrat Ali, a cousin of the Prophet and Islam's fourth caliph, who was yet to return from battle, she asks Sugra of his whereabouts. Sugra is a parrot, a messenger in Sanskrit classics, who is also prominent in Awadhi. The Prophet's daughter tells the parrot to go hunt for Ali Saheb and says, 'If you can't find him anywhere, you must go to Vrindavan.' In our poetry, language and culture, we were very much integrated. Much of this had come from Sufiism. The Sufis and the Shias were first cousins in the sense that they were both sects derived from Ali's pre-eminence. So, this is the way things were going in the 1940s.

My father had set up a practice in Lucknow. He even got a job in Lakhimpur Kheri where I may have lived for a while too. I remember my circumcision ceremony was held there. We were in these places for a little bit, but our home was always Mustafabad. That was where we always retreated to. As we grew older, there was a debate about where to send us, the children, to school.

One part of the family said, 'We will not send our children to English schools. We have been fighting them. We have our culture. Why should we corrupt the children with English?' Then the writing on the wall was shown to them, and they made a compromise. So, my three brothers and I were sent to La Martinière College in Lucknow. It was a fantastic school. This must have been 1947.

Meanwhile, Panditji had told us there would be no partition. Everything depended on Panditji. My father's elder brother, Wazir Naqvi, was the first Congress MLA from Raebareli. All of them were very, very sceptical about Partition. They did not want it, nor did they think it was going to happen. I still remember those conversations.

They romanticized Jinnah as a persona. He was a good-looking man. His sartorial detail was exemplary, he smoked cigars, and they thought he was a clever fellow. They also thought that even Jinnah himself was not interested in Pakistan – he was just using the demand as a bargaining chip. Nevertheless, in my family, Panditji was numero uno, and no one could match him. He had promised us there would be no Partition, and so it was taken for granted that it wouldn't happen. Then when Partition took place, the elders looked at each other and said, 'Panditji must have been under some pressure; there must have been a good reason', and so they were willing to forgive him.

Land reforms were an important part of the Congress party's strategy. Panditji said our land would not be taken away. He said Hindus had taken to Western education like ducks to water. Muslims were standing still with their Urdu and Urdu culture. They had, therefore, not been able to create a middle class.

We thought what Panditji was saying was that since we did not have a middle class they would delay land reforms as far as we were concerned, until we built one. People from inner cities were crossing over to cantonments and civil lines neighbourhoods, and the Hindu middle class was urbanizing, educating themselves in English and finding employment. This transition was much more rapid among Hindus and was very tardy among Muslims. They liked their inner cities, because they liked their Urdu, and they liked their culture. They forgot there were important things like putting bread on the table.

I don't remember 15 August 1947 very well. My uncle, the Congressman, held a little meeting in his own house, where a flag was unfurled. All the local and some state Congress functionaries came. I think I was asked to recite something.

Partition was very ugly. It was a very big tragedy. A family got divided and was fooled. This part of the discussion is missing from our literature: they were told that this was temporary. They were reassured that we would all come together. An uncle of mine was a captain in the army. My mother's youngest sister was married to him. Come Partition, and he was wondering where to go.

They took out a tape measure, and they measured the distance on the map between Bombay and Mustafabad, and Karachi and Mustafabad. It was almost the same. So don't worry, they told the family. In Karachi, brigadier so and so is known to us, that's good for us professionally, and nothing else will be any different anyway.

This was how decisions were made. No one went to Pakistan for great ideological reasons. The thing that people don't know today is that only Punjab was divided. Leave Bengal aside for now. People from Lahore came to Amritsar, Ludhiana and Delhi. And Muslims from only those parts – Ludhiana, Jalandhar and Amritsar – went over to that side. The only transfer of power was in Punjab. The rest of us did not know what happened.

My family, especially, was in shock during all this because Panditji had told us there would be no partition. We stood where we were. My mother's two sisters were married in Pakistan. Why? There weren't many Sayyid boys of proper education and pedigree available here! This was a big thing then. Also, since they would not study English, there was a whole line of people in the community who were PhDs in

Urdu, which had begun to diminish in value in India. So, these were unemployed PhDs who would not go to Pakistan because they were ideologically opposed to it.

Then in the CPI, Joshi was replaced by B.T. Ranadive. He was called the 'Stalin of the Party', and he said that class war, on a revolutionary scale, was possible in Pakistan. It was a hint to all the Muslim comrades from here to start finding a way to go there. This gave some of them the ideological justification to go across. One of them was a dear uncle of mine, S.M. Naseer. He had gone to jail in Kanpur for his revolutionary work. When he went to Pakistan, he found that he was unable to get a visa to come to India. I was by then an influential journalist, and I could get people visas. But even I was finding it difficult to help him procure one to come here for weddings, funerals, etc.

Once, twice, thrice. No dice. I went to the highest level to find out why he was repeatedly denied permission to travel. It turned out that the CID report that the British had prepared for him was exceedingly harsh. And this report was now with the intelligence wing of the Indian High Commission. And they wouldn't give him the visa because he was deemed to be a dangerous fellow. For seventeen years he couldn't come to India. Then, finally, he managed to come for my daughter's wedding. The irony was that he eventually became friends with a fellow who was in the Indian CID in Karachi, the same fellow who had given him that terrible report.

I finished Senior Cambridge in 1959. We stayed in the school dormitories for a while, and then we became day scholars. Lucknow became home, and Mustafabad remained our anchor. Mustafabad was not just a home, it was the centre of our lives, and it occupied our dreams. We found every excuse to go there. For holidays, during the mango season. Over the years, of course, as lands were sold off and the elders started fading out, the visits decreased. We still have a shell of a haveli there, which my sister now looks after.

One detail that might be interesting is that while the four brothers were sent to La Martiniere, the two sisters were sent to an Islamic school. There, the women – as in Hindu society – were given the charge of protecting culture, as defined by religion and religious rituals. It created a kind of apartheid within the family. We had separate books, separate friends, separate interests. It took a toll, and it took us a while to rediscover each other. But what a magnificent rediscovery it has been.

We were very optimistic about our future. La Martinière exerted a great deal of influence on us. And it was a very English school. There was no difference between the communities in the school, but there was a little distance from ritual and religion. Nehru himself had that. This distance was derived from a need that was created in order to build an integrated society. But it would find itself out of sync with the India as it has evolved today. In other words, between us and the mofussil, which came to power subsequently, there is a difference. Liberalism did come, to a certain extent, from our westernized education. Moreover,

Urdu itself was an extremely eclectic Catholic culture. Once you came under the canopy of Urdu, religious differences completely evaporated.

The setting and the languages of North India were Awadhi, Braj Bhasha, Maithili and Bhojpuri. Somehow, because of the elegant urbanity of Urdu, the new emerging leadership thought that these languages are 'gavaar' (illiterate) languages. Can you believe it? This is how inferiority complexes build and nations built on inferiority complexes are always brittle. You can't describe Tulsidas, who wrote in Awadhi, as gavaar. Was there a greater poet? This is a problem that arose through the agency of a gentleman called Bharatendu Harishchandra. The Hindi, Hindu, Hindustani movement was started by him. Although he himself was a Persian poet, he always thought that the Hindu must culturally have an urbane language. Folksiness was confused for boorishness. Which it is not. That was the sad part. And all that continues till today. We have this renaming, redigging business because of this. These are the acts of small men.

I was a very naughty boy, but I was a talented and popular one. Before the Senior Cambridge examination, there used to be an internal examination to see how many of us were going to disgrace the school. If we disgraced the teachers entirely, they would not let us appear for the exams. Mr Law was our teacher. And there was me with my answer booklet. In the physics paper, there was a question on Newton's laws. Arre, baap re baap! I had no idea. So, I wrote, and I quote:

On everything that Newton saw,
He always made some stupid law.
This line is bent, that line is straight,
When bodies sink, they lose their weight.
The air consists of oxygen,
The types of food consumed by men,
In brief, on everything he looked,
A new and tedious law he cooked.

Did I make this up? Yes! Right there. And I submitted it. When the results came, on the day of reckoning, people got hundred, ninety, eighty, whatever. And finally! 'Here's a boy who's fit to be a mochi (cobbler),' said Mr Law. But he had a sense of humour, because for this poem – which was the only thing I had written on that paper – he gave me ten upon hundred. (*Laughs uproariously.*)

I finished Senior Cambridge and was loafing around. I was becoming very popular in Lucknow. Hazratganj became my haunt. I got great grades in Senior Cambridge, but then reports of my not being on the straight and narrow – much like Lord Krishna and his pranks – started reaching my father. He thought that it was time to pack me off. A big black box was procured, in which my clothes were packed. I was given a black sherwani. My friend Safdar came to the railway station to see me off. I was sent off to Aligarh Muslim University with caution money of one hundred and eighty rupees.

I was put in the hostel, where on jummah (Friday), a boy

came up and said, 'Salaam alaikum, chaliye tayyar ho jaiye, namaz ka waqt hai' (It's time for the prayer). I had never experienced this in my home. So, first, I did not go for namaz, and instead walked up and down in great consternation. Then came my aunt, Agatha. She was my uncle's younger sister. She was a firebrand leader of the Lucknow University Students' Federation, therefore, a communist, and had a PhD degree. She heard I was in AMU and thought my father was making me into a Muslim. She came and said, 'Chalo yahaan se' (Get out of here). My god, I was waiting for that. I immediately packed my bags and left the place.

Then I came to Delhi, but I didn't know where I could go. All the admissions were over.

Aunt Agatha knew Dr K.M. Ashraf who was a remarkable historian. He wrote the history of the people, the first subaltern study. Obviously, he was also a communist. He was then the head of the Department of History at Kirori Mal College. Now, everything about that college was good, expect for its name; I was a little averse to it.

Dr Ashraf put me in touch with a man called Frank Thakurdas. He was a wonderful teacher of political science. He was from Government College, Lahore. He saw me, sized me up and took me to his friend, Professor Madan of St Stephen's College. He was the head of the Department of English. Madan said, 'Haven't you come a couple of months too late?' Still, I filled an application form and left it there. My uncle, the communist, stayed in a two-room apartment in Joshi Path in Karol Bagh. What an intellectual influence he was on me.

My uncle couldn't afford this two-room house, so one room was taken up by Professor Nand Lal Dhar. Can you see the secularism we enjoyed? A Muslim couple from Mustafabad and a Kashmiri Hindu living in a poky apartment in Delhi. And I was fitted in there, somewhere. I stayed there with him for a while and then came away to Lucknow thinking even if I disliked the name, I'll go to Kirori Mal College.

Meanwhile, in Lucknow, a letter had come for me from St Stephen's College. My uncle, being very much a gentleman, did not open it. He waited for me to come. It was my admission letter! But it was too late. The date for accepting the admission had passed. I missed out on a year of college. I spent that as a complete and total loafer in Lucknow, a vagabond, busy falling in love and writing poetry. Then I came back to Kirori Mal and finished college from there.

After that I borrowed a suit from my brother-in-law and went and met the Englishman who was the Resident Editor of the *Statesman*. He made me sit in a corner and write four hundred words on mangoes, which I did. Then I got a letter offering me a paid apprenticeship for three hundred rupees a month.

This was in 1965. I went running to my friend who was working in *Hindustan Times* and said, 'Listen, I had applied for a job in Air India and they are giving me seven hundred rupees. Should I take that?' He said, 'You idiot, this is the best newspaper job in the world.' I stayed, and I did very well.

I was posted by the *Statesman* to Rajasthan. Sumohan Lal Sukhadia was the chief minister at the time. I was sitting in my guest house with a bottle of beer and writing my piece. I thought that with beer one's sentences flowed more easily. I happened to look out of the window and spotted Sukhadia crying. I asked him what had happened. He said that Panditji had died. The first thing I did, almost as a knee-jerk reaction, was pour out my beer into the sink. And we cried. Our adoration for him had grown. Of course, we were also very critical. There were many things Panditji did because of which we continue to suffer even today. Some of these things he did knowingly; some, unknowingly. But until his death, Jawaharlal Nehru was the undisputed leader of the Indian Muslims. That is true.

Through most of my life, I had not faced many troubles being a Muslim in India. Yes, there was one issue. The problem was that Aruna, my wife, and I could not find a house. Negotiations would go up to a point, they would hear our name, and they wouldn't give us a house. This was in the 1960s. This continues to happen in 2022, of course. Ultimately, some friends intervened, and we found a place. This is how it went on. In the 1980s, my relatives from Pakistan used to visit us and envy me. They used to ask, 'How can I buy land here?' That was until 1989–90. Today, they pity me.

The seeds of it were there from the beginning, but we never saw them. What did Panditji tell us? No partition. It happened. Panditji had said no zamindari abolition. It happened. Panditji turned out to be a virtuous young man who played the piano in a brothel without knowing what was going on upstairs.

———•———

It was now (early 1947) increasingly apparent even to Jawaharlal that Pakistan, in some form, would have to be created; the League was simply not going to work with Congress in a united government of India. He, nonetheless, tried to prod leaders of the League into discussions on the new arrangements, which he still hoped would fall short of an absolute partition. By early March, as communal rioting continued across northern India, even this hope had faded. Both Patel and Nehru agreed that, despite the Mahatma's refusal to contemplate such a prospect, Congress had no alternative but to agree and partition Punjab and Bengal; the option of a loose Indian union including a quasi-sovereign Pakistan would neither be acceptable to the League nor result in a viable government for the rest of India. By the time Mountbatten arrived on 24 March 1947, the die had been cast. It was he, however, who rapidly ended the game altogether. [1]

———•———

The backroom boys were Babu Jagjivan Ram, Rajendra Prasad and Sardar Patel. And they were in for a Hindu India. Kazim Raza, a relative of mine, was the DIG of Police in Delhi. Come 1947, he went to Govind Ballah Pant (freedom fighter and first Chief Minister of Uttar Pradesh), and said it was his turn to be IG of Police. Pant said, 'Come, sit down. We have created a country there. And it is important for us that that country not collapse. Your talents are required much more there than they are required here.' Kazim Raza got the hint – he went to Pakistan and retired as the chief of Pakistan intelligence.

What do I think is the future of this country? Well, we are going to go through it. They can't turn this country into a Hindu Rashtra, I don't think so. The tragedy of the cow belt should not be superimposed on this nation. If we could become a Hindu Rashtra, then at least there would be peace at the end of it. But since we cannot, we are in for constant travails.

8

A Coming of Age

Ravindra Pandya grew up in Baroda. He worked in Coca-Cola before starting his own business ventures. He has two daughters. He is seventy-nine years old.

I was born in Balaghat, a town in Madhya Pradesh, on 13 September 1942. We are Gujaratis, but our forefathers had settled in Madhya Pradesh. My father was born and raised in a town known as Hatta and then moved to Benares. After college, he went to the UK for the ICS. He couldn't clear the examination, but he completed his BA (Hons) from London University. He was awarded the Fulbright Scholarship in 1955 and taught History at the University of Chicago. He then returned to India and did his MA from Allahabad.

When I was two months old, my father got a job in Baroda, and we relocated to Gujarat where we have lived since. My father worked in the Pratap Singh Rao College of Commerce and Economics. Later it became a part of MS University. He was the first registrar of the university and the first dean of history and arts. Though he taught history, he was also an expert in Sanskrit and Hindi literature.

My mother came from a town called Chhindwara in Madhya Pradesh. Since she lost her mother at a very young age, she studied in a residential school in Benaras, which was run by the Theosophical Society. Her father was the first Indian chief conservator of forests, working for the British. He was the principal of the Balaghat Forest School and was awarded an MBE by the British. He too was originally from a very poor family. Her father and his brother studied under street lamps. When they grew up, my grandfather became the chief conservator and his brother, a very famous lawyer. They became one of the richest people in the community.

The two brothers decided to start a scholarship to support poor students from the community. The deal was that the students availing the scholarship did not have to return the money but instead have to pay it forward and help educate other students. And as it turned out, one of these scholarship students was my father! My father came from a very poor family. When he joined college in Benares, he took arts because the fee was five rupees for arts and seven rupees for science. He was good at studies. In those days, the names of those who graduated were published in the gazette. I have a copy of it with me.

I grew up on the university campus in Baroda among artists, poets, historians and visiting foreign delegates. When I was sixteen, my father died of cancer after struggling with the disease for a year and a half. He was only forty-four. He got cancer in spite of the fact that he used to walk for more than twelve kilometres a day, was a strict vegetarian, never drank tea or coffee or ate excessive spices. He was a pious man. He had seen the world and also written three books.

In those days, there was no medical aid. All the money that he had saved up until his illness – which was largely from his salary and the money he earned by correcting examination papers (four rupees and twelve anna per paper!) – was used in his treatment. I still have the bills totalling up to fifty-eight thousand rupees from Bombay Hospital.

When my father died, there was no money in our house except seven thousand rupees that was given to our family upon his death by the inusrance company. Luckily, the university was a small, close-knit community. My mother had studied until Intermediate. She was given a job as the superintendent of the ladies' hostel, which had just been built. She was thirty-nine at the time. Unlike other widows at the time, she did not return to her parents' home. This job gave her a secure place to stay. My sister lived with her, but because I was a boy I had to stay in the boys' hostel. Our books and school fees were taken care of by the university. Whatever I am today is because of the university.

I don't remember much about Independence Day. I was still so young. But I think some sweets were made in our house on that day. I do, however, remember the early years of independence. Maharaja Pratap Singh Rao Gaekwad of Baroda was reluctant to accede to the Indian Union. There is an exhibition ground known as Pradarshan Maidan in Baroda and Sardar Patel had come there and spoken at a public meeting. I remember that. I would have been five or six. I am not sure whether I went to the talk with my parents or if it was recounted to me.

The maharaja of Baroda was one of the most forward-looking rulers of the time. He was Maharashtrian, and the area was predominantly occupied by the Marathi community. He made water reservoirs that used to serve nearly one lakh people in those days. There was compulsory education. Girls went to school for free. The *Gazette of Baroda* was published in the Devanagari and Gujarati scripts because the ruler was Maharashtrian and the subjects were Gujarati. That way, both could read it. Of the three clock towers in Baroda, two have markings in Devanagari.

By 1947 or 1948, I had also started school. I used to take a bus to get to school. We had a neighbour, who was my father's colleague. Their daughter used to take me with her. She was older to me by seven or eight years and was very pretty. I remember people used to be nice to me because of her. (*Laughs.*)

I also remember when Gandhiji died. The area we were living in was called Dandia Bazaar, which was predominantly Maharashtrian and Brahmin, and it witnessed a lot of riots. Godse had a relative called Abhyankar who lived in Baroda. They had a shop. I think they used to sell cement and things like that. That shop was burnt in the riots. I saw this with my own eyes. A mob came and burnt it. In front of our house

lived a Dr Joshi, who was our family GP. That evening, a
man – who had been badly beaten up – was brought to him.
I remember the bloodied body being carried inside. Then the
police came and dispersed the crowd.

———————•———————

Riots broke out in various parts of the country as the news
of Gandhi's death spread. *The New York Times* reported
fifteen people dead on the following day.[1] Communal
tempers were still very high, and people were just beginning
to process the trauma of Partition. *The Guardian* newspaper
in the UK wrote:

> News of Gandhi's death was announced by the All-India
> Radio at six o'clock and a crowd of several thousands
> immediately gathered at Birla House. The crowd was
> tense but subdued, and its mood appeared to be one of
> stunned sorrow.

> Repercussions of the crime are certain to be widespread
> and intense throughout India and Pakistan. It may
> produce that change of heart for which Gandhi
> laboured and gave his life. On the other hand, it may
> stimulate communal frenzy; the presence of 5,000,000
> Hindu and Sikh refugees from Pakistan (of whom
> about 400,000 are in Delhi) has exacerbated public
> tempers and communal organisations such as the Hindu

Mahasabha and Rashtriya Swayam Sewak Sangh have
been active in preaching vengeance against Pakistan.[2]

———————•———————

Up until my father's death, I used to be a playful boy, a
mischievous teenager. I used to get punished for something
or the other every day. I never came back home without
scraping my knees or tearing my clothes. I never thought
about the future. But when my father died, I was jolted
into adulthood. My father's death brought all our relatives
together. They all felt that I would have to be enrolled in the
police school in Junagadh and trained to become a police
constable because I was a good-for-nothing. They didn't see
any other future for me. Unfortunately for them, I was the
one who ended up giving employment to their children a
few years later!

I graduated in psychology from MS University. In those
days, I used to stay in a hostel, and my professor was my
father's colleague. His son was three years senior to me. He
was my mentor and guide. They had relatives in Delhi who
visited Baroda for their holidays every year. When I was
about to graduate, this gentleman said, 'Come to Delhi, I'll
get you a job.' He worked at the Coca-Cola Company and
gave me a job there. I joined the communication department.

My eyes really opened when I took up a job and started
living in Delhi. That is where my vision was broadened.

Coming from a small town, you can't imagine the scale and complexity of the country. I was a real country bumpkin. I didn't even know how to knot a tie!

Delhi's culture was different. There were friends who were your good friends from the first of the month to the seventh or so. After that they'd disappear, only to reappear again on the first of the following month. My uncle was a brigadier in the army, and I stayed with him initially before moving out. My salary was three hundred and fifty rupees, which was a huge sum of money at the time. I could live like a king.

I married in 1970. My wife adapted to Delhi life quite quickly. There was a small, but vibrant, Gujarati community in Delhi, and our life revolved around exploring hotels and clubs, social events and soaking up new experiences. It was a memorable time.

At that time, many young adults were migrating to the US or the UK. Due to my work experience in Coca-Cola, I had lots of offers from these countries, but I never thought of going there. I was happy here. My mother and sister were in Baroda, and I was in Delhi. It was a happy time for me. I would have loved to travel, but in those days getting foreign exchange was difficult and getting a passport took six months.

After working in Coca-Cola for several years, I became an entrepreneur and returned to Baroda. My wife was a teacher, and we have two daughters. Like my mother, my wife too is a strong woman and our goal was to educate our daughters well. If I look back and think of my early working life, I see a lot of difference. Now I think, people are not committed to work.

'Me first, country next' is the attitude that most people have. In my time, we were proud of our country. Priorities have changed. We have become self-centred. We don't think beyond our family. We have become more regressive than progressive.

Both my girls have had arranged marriages, but outside our community. Our experience with members of our community put us off. We were taken aback by the attitudes of people who were rude just because we only had daughters. Potential suitors and their families would come home and then ask things like 'Your property will go to your daughters only, right?' or 'Your children wear jeans?' The lowest point was when a relative said 'We will come to your house but we will not even drink water because you have two daughters.'

We were educated and well travelled, and my work involved interacting with people from all strata of society. We had evolved, but the community had stuck to its regressive ways. Therefore, we looked for sons-in-law who were compatible with our outlook rather than compatible with the community.

Overall, at the level of the country too, we have regressed. I think in the 1960s and 1970s we were more progressive in our ideas. Of course, there were always riots in the country. But now there are riots for selfish reasons not public causes. (*Laughs.*) We used to have a lively life. Now I am nearly eighty, and our lives have become quite isolated.

My dream for India is that we should be proud of the country. India has talent and a very rich culture. Our name around the world is flying high at the moment, but we should be self-sufficient in matters of food, education and healthcare. Somehow, our story continues to be about roti, kapda aur makaan, though several decades have passed since independence. Yet, the struggle continues.

9

A Long Way Home

Sahib Singh Virdi *came to India after the Partition. He retired as a brigadier from the Indian Army's Corps of Engineers. He is ninety years old and lives in Chandigarh.*

I was born in Gharota Kalan in Gurdaspur district on 6 February 1932. It was the first posting of my father, Dr Man Singh, who had graduated from King Edward Medical College, Lahore in 1928. He got married in May 1929 and moved to Gharota Kalan, where we stayed till 1937. As a government doctor, my father ran the local rural dispensary.

My parents had four children in Gharota Kalan. I was the second. We were all born from 1930 onwards, at regular intervals of one and a half years. There was no family planning at that time. (*Laughs.*) Four more children were born subsequently. At the time of Partition, my elder sister was seventeen, and I was fifteen and a half, and the third sibling was fourteen. The rest were all small kids, not even teenagers.

By 1938, my father had learnt the art – and it was an art – of being an eye surgeon. Blindness and eye diseases were rampant in Punjab then, especially cataracts and trachoma. My father was a great admirer of Bal Gangadhar Tilak, and it was as a response to his call that he decided to devote his life to establishing an eye surgery practice in the smallest of villages. At the time, there were only three or four eye surgeons in the whole of Punjab, which meant an area covering present-day Haryana, Himachal Pradesh, Punjab in India and Punjab in Pakistan. Resources were extremely limited, and my father wanted to serve the people. Over and above the eye practice, he also carried out other types of general surgeries.

In 1937, we moved to another place, across the river Ravi, to a village called Maingri or Nurkot. This was a Muslim-dominated area. Gurdaspur district had four tehsils, three to the south of the Ravi, and one to the north. We stayed there for about a year and thereafter, in 1938, moved to Gorala Lallian. This is the area that is now connected by the Kartarpur Corridor. We stayed there until Partition. Here too, my father established a rural dispensary and – despite limited resources – an eye centre as well.

The rural dispensary, which my father developed into an eye hospital with the help of the local population, was in the middle of a large field. Barring the staff, which included two compounders, sometimes one, nobody else lived nearby. We were a couple of kilometres away from the nearest neighbour. The place was absolutely open.

My father loved gardens and growing flowers, and he tended to one outside the hospital. The aim of the whole enterprise was simply to be of service to these people who had such poor access to even basic infrastructure and healthcare. We were a service-minded people then – we gave up ourselves for the community.

In Gorala Lallian, as I had said, there was plenty of open space. With very little funds, my father created huge sheds where he would carry out cataract surgeries. Kashmiri labourers used to make mud walls for two annas a day, and these would be topped with a simple roof. Nowadays, cataract operations are done in five minutes – it's a very simple procedure with all the technology that is available. But in those days you had to be hospitalized for eight days after surgery, and patients needed great post-operative care. My father needed help. So, he trained me and my brother – even though we were small kids – to help him in the hospital.

The place was far away from everywhere and not connected by a national highway or any such road. In fact, dirt tracks led to the village. Only a railway line ran past it, where one train would go in the morning and the same train would return in the evening. It had only two compartments.

You could hear the whistle of the train from a distance, and we often kept time by it. There were no watches either. My father had a horse. He would go from village to village on horseback. His assistant would hold his medical bag and follow him. The water was so filthy, he would take potassium permanganate and put it in buckets and throw it in the wells. There were no hand pumps, and the water could have been contaminated at times.

My father gave lectures to the local villagers on hygiene, sanitation, etc. That was service. People were so far away from civilization in these places that many of them hadn't even seen a bus! I never saw a bus myself as a child. Once when we went with my father to Amritsar, we saw buses and wondered what they were! There were no cars, obviously. Not even in Amritsar. Back then only the British and rich Indians or officials had cars.

Everything was self-contained in the villages. Everything was grown locally. All tradesmen were in the village too, or at best in the adjoining village. Cotton was grown and spun there. We never interacted with the outside world. My father was offered an option to join the armed forces as a doctor, but he refused. He said he would serve his own people. It was a time where that sort of spirit endured. People really loved him. You will see how they paid us back, when I tell you about Partition.

So, we stayed there. But then what about all of us children? My elder sister and the one who was just after me couldn't go to school since there was no education for girls in the village. They were put in a hostel in Gurdaspur, far away. My father was a stickler for good clothes. The local Muslims were very good at tailoring. He hired a tailor and got twill shirts and khaki trousers made for us. We were the envy of the village. (*Laughs.*) People would talk to each other and say, 'Look at Doctor Saheb's children, they are so well turned out.'

But – and there is a big but – there was no school there. Whatever passed for a school was only up to Class 4 and whatever teaching was done was imparted in Urdu. We sat under a big banyan tree, and the person who taught us was also an adhoc postmaster for all the villages in the area. He would come with a mailbag filled with letters, money orders and packages. The teachers would sort them out and give them to the boys from the various villages to deliver on their way home! That was the way.

Like I told you, there weren't too many wells with clean water. Many people would come and take water from the village pond. Can you believe it? They washed animals there, they bathed themselves there and drank the water too. Sometimes, water collected in pools in the rainy season, and that water too was used for household activities, because, as I mentioned earlier, there were no hand pumps. I don't think you can even imagine what life was like then.

Only the hospital had two hand pumps. The people were so poor. At our so-called school, we just sat and repeated whatever the teacher said. Children wore all kinds of scraps and ends to school. Some came in kachhas (thin cotton shorts); others wore scraps of dhoti, whatever they could find and their families could scrape together. Sikh boys would tie a joora (knotted hair); there was no cloth to tie a turban. No one had any shoes. And we all just sat there repeating what the teacher said.

In order to compensate for our lack of exposure to the world, my father subscribed to a lot of newspapers and magazines. *The Tribune* used to be published from Lahore. Then there was the *Civil and Military Gazette*, which was published from Karachi. Both these newspapers would reach us three or four days late. But we used to read them and, in a way, know what was happening around the world.

I was very fond of reading. Even in my father's time, most schools taught only in Urdu. But he had studied in Khalsa College, Amritsar, and he knew Punjabi and could read the Gurmukhi script. There were some fine magazines in Punjabi, such as *Preet Lari* and *Phulwari*. There was also a children's magazine called *Balak* and a weekend magazine called *Junior*. We used to get all these by post. We would bind all the issues, published through the year, and save them for later. We had, for what was available in that place at that time, a reasonably good library. They occupied two shelves in our house. But you know even with all these limitations, we were quite aware of the environment in the country and what was happening around us.

Only the very privileged possessed cycles. My father had one, but where could he ride it? There were no paved roads, only bullock cart tracks. The most important possession was a horse. As kids, we spent all day outside – in the mud, in the fields. We participated in races and jumping matches. All in the mud. What about in winter, you ask? (*Laughs.*) In those days, people didn't feel cold.

At the time, everyone was an admirer of Germany. We thought of them as hardy people, and we wanted to be like them. In winter, the temperature of the area was around zero degree, but I used to get up at 4 a.m., massage my body with mustard oil and then have a cold water bath. Boys used to come with one kurta and no shoes! Cotton was the only fabric used. There were no woollens or silks.

My mother had some silks, of course. But even in the harshest of winters, village boys walked around in simple khaddar kurtas. My father had three-piece suits. But once Gandhi announced the Swadeshi movement, he stopped wearing them. My mother wasn't allowed to wear any jewellery. Everyone spun their own yarn and made their own fabric. And we would make chaddar, like a sheet, from it. That's all we wore. Even in the harshest of winters.

We had a small plank of wood called takhti. We would take it to the village pond, rub clay on it and make things of terracotta with it. These were household things, used for everyday living. We made our own pens and fashioned our ink from the black soot of the diyas. The pen was usually reed. Everyone used to carry a small knife.

English was taught from Class 5 but, of course, we didn't have a school. Eight kilometres away was a small town called Kanjrur Dattan. There was a respected community of Hindus called Mohyal Brahmins because of which the town had a DAV School, established on the ideals of Dayanand

Saraswati. I couldn't attend school for Class 5, for some reason. Therefore, a teacher was engaged to come home and teach me. I joined DAV School in Class 6.

You will be surprised that during my career I worked in the Corps of Engineers in the Indian Army, and people used to praise me for my knowledge of engineering, but the school I went to had classes in neither science nor drawing. English was basic, and everything else was in Urdu.

In DAV School, they had a weekly havan, and they recited the Gayatri Mantra one hundred and eight times. The mantras were written in a small booklet called *Mantron ka Qaida*, and guess what – it was in Urdu! I was very poor in mathematics. I didn't know English at all. To be honest, because my father was an important person, some special treatment was given to me.

Most students travelled by foot. My cousin in Amritsar had a cycle with no tyres. So, I fashioned my own tyres for the cycle. We used to repair everything ourselves. I went to school on this cycle. En route, I had to cross a river. I would carry the cycle on my shoulders, wade through the water and ride again on the other side. It used to take me about an hour to reach school on foot and about thirty minutes by cycle.

It was a very strict school. They believed in the philosophy of 'spare the rod and spoil the child'. I remember the teachers used to carry sticks around to hit us with. Once, I got a severe beating on my hand, and the pain lasted for months! Similarly, I remember, in high school a teacher caught hold of my ears and lifted me off the ground! My ear started bleeding. But I was so scared that I never complained to my father. It caused a lifelong impairment.

Like I said, we were aware of what was going on in the rest of the country. We would follow the latest news on the freedom struggle. We worshipped the Congress then. Parbodh Chander was the Gurdaspur legislator, and he was underground; as were most of the politicians and political activists. There was also a chap called Dileep Singh Tipyala who was the head of the Communist Party of Punjab.

My father had similar sympathies. He too believed in 'for the people, by the people'. Tipyala Saheb would come to our house in the middle of the night, have a meal with my father and then give me a lecture on communism. We admired white people – especially Germans – because they were so technologically advanced. And in many ways we were grateful to the British. Before them, was there a postal system? No. Was there a transport system? No. Was there any telegraph service? No. Were there any roads? No. In order to govern us, the British created these services.

Punjab was a place where the water depth was sixty feet below the ground. How did you bring water out from such depth? People struggled in the state. It was a place of great famines. Who created the biggest irrigation system in Punjab? The British constructed the first Upper Ganges Canal in 1845. And, thereafter, wherever the British went, they set up these canals.

We were aware and grateful for what the British

brought to us, but we also wanted a free country. Both were concurrent. It was a taboo to speak English. I was a graduate in mathematics and physics when I joined the elite military academy, but I couldn't utter a word of English. Because we never spoke the language. Nowadays, English is the mother tongue in which we speak Punjabi. (*Laughs.*)

So, anyway, to come back to the point, we were all very excited about the freedom movement. We discussed it often and at length. There were jalsas (demonstrations) in many parts of the state, and the leaders were often put behind bars. Some of them would come over and talk to us boys. We loved our leaders; we respected them. We used to stand for hours to catch a glimpse of them. Nationalist fervour was a potent potion. We all wanted to be Bhagat Singh. We wanted the British to go! Well, no. We wanted to throw them out. And above all, we loved Gandhi and Nehru. We were totally star-struck by those two men.

As we neared 1947, our fervour only increased. Jinnah was not respected by anybody. Around that time, Punjab was ruled by the Unionist Party. The Muslim League did not even have a foothold in the state. We really hated Jinnah. We thought he was a toady of the British.

We heard about the possibility of partition from the newspapers. Punjabi newspapers were very critical of the prospect of splitting the state into two on communal lines. Initially, I thought that partition would never happen, and that these were just things being talked about to create confusion about India's independence. The situation was fraught for the British after Churchill was defeated and Attlee came to power.

The naval mutiny had just happened. A large number of Indian soldiers were also drafted into the British Indian Army for the Second World War. They were a well-trained force. Potentially India had a great armed force. They were all prepared to fight to death. The British were scared. They had to evolve a plan in which they could utilize Indians to fight against Indians. They wanted to prove to us, Indians, that we could not administer ourselves.

That is why they sent Mountbatten. Do you know what Radcliffe said about Mountbatten? He is supposed to have said 'Mountbatten was such a crooked chap that if he swallowed a piece of wire at dinner time, it would come out as a corkscrew in the morning.' (*Laughs.*) Pardon me, if the joke is in poor taste and your sensibilities are delicate.

What did Radcliffe himself know anyway? He was paid some three thousand-odd pounds to come to India and draw the line of partition. Now, a man who does not know anything about the anatomy of this country, a man who does not know the type of people who reside there, the religions they follow, their places of worship, the system of irrigation and power supply, what can such a man do. He was totally ignorant about anything to do with India. Anyway, what is the point of getting angry about it now. At the time, we were so sure that partition was just a bogeyman the British were using that the news of Radcliffe's appointment came as a bolt from the blue.

I had finished my matriculation exams on 7 March 1947. By then, the riots had already begun. In fact, a large number of examination centres witnessed Hindu–Muslim riots. I wanted to join college in either Lahore or Amritsar. I would have liked to join Khalsa College, Amritsar. It was my dream.

The building of Khalsa College itself is so beautiful; nothing like that existed in most of the world. It's a lovely college that was originally planned by the British because they wanted to have a rung of officers who would carry on governance on their behalf. In my father's time the entire staff of the college was sent from the UK. My father's elder brother had built a house opposite the college – a modern house, like the ones in Chandigarh. The aim was that I would study at Khalsa College and choose medicine or engineering.

The British game plan was never leaked to anybody. When the plan of partition was rejected by the Sikhs, Master Tara Singh was the leader of the Sikhs. He went and tore down the flag from the pole. We got news that things were not working out the way we thought they would. They initially wanted to partition India in 1948. Then they must have thought that it was best to advance the date.

———————●———————

Mountbatten pulled the date of 15 August for 'Transfer of Power' out of his hat. It was not a significant date for the two countries, but it was significant for him. He was asked the question of the date at a press conference, and he blurted out 15 August because it was the day the Japanese Empire surrendered during the Second World War.

Mountbatten was later quoted as saying:

> The date I chose came out of the blue. I chose it in reply to a question. I was determined to show I was master of the whole event. When they asked had we set a date, I knew it had to be soon. I hadn't worked it out exactly then – I thought it had to be about August or September and I then went out to the 15th August. Why? Because it was the second anniversary of Japan's surrender.[1]

As soon as the date was announced, astrologers around India got to work. The overwhelming response was that the date was inauspicious. Several of them wrote to Mountbatten asking that the date be changed. Mountbatten was quite frustrated by this. In his personal report to the King, he wrote:

> The astrologers are being rather tiresome since both the 13th and the 15th have been declared inauspicious days, whereas the 14th is auspicious. I was not warned that I ought to consult the astrologers before fixing the day for the transfer of power, but luckily, this has been got over by the Constituent Assembly deciding to meet before midnight on the auspicious 14th and take over power as midnight strikes which is apparently still an auspicious moment.[2]

Then Radcliffe was called, and he was put in charge of making the new borders. The Survey of India office is in Dehradun. There, Radcliffe accessed all the maps of the country, and he drew a line partitioning India. Nobody knew where the line was. We knew that Nehru and Jinnah had agreed to the two-state proposal, but Gandhi never approved of it. Really speaking, we did not know any details of the proposal. Where was the line going to be? Would this be in India or Pakistan? Would we be in India or Pakistan? No idea. Can you imagine looking at a future like this? We knew that it was in the offing. But in every respect we were totally taken by surprise.

In August 1947, I was at home in Gorala Lallian. I was getting ready to pack my bags and go to college. We heard that independence would come. But even on 14 August we did not know that the country would be declared independent the next day. How would we know? Our newspapers came three or four days late!

There was no radio and no other means of gathering information. Did we hear Nehru's speech? We didn't even know Nehru was speaking. See, you must understand our circumstances. We were in a remote place. We never imagined that the people who were living there for centuries would have to shift lock, stock and barrel overnight.

Let me tell you what happened. Although independence, and the formation of Pakistan, was announced on 15 August, at least where we were, people were not aware of the line of partition. Gurdaspur was a Muslim-majority district. On 23

August, more than a week after Independence Day, at about 1 p.m., we heard rifle shots from the villages all around the hospital. Wounded people started arriving, and then almost all villages were set on fire, and smoke was billowing to the sky all around us.

Initially, my father had organized care of the wounded but, as the day progressed, he too became worried and collected all of us – my mother, four brothers and three sisters – and made us hide in a corn field because he was not sure if the hospital would get attacked. My youngest sister was three years old at the time.

Other people in the village were also not sure of what to do and where to go, and so, naturally, they came to my father to seek his advice. He too had no way of knowing what was happening, so everyone thought it was best to move to Kanjrur Dattan, a big town about eight kilometres away, where I went to school. We had a couple of Christian employees whom we entrusted with our home and possessions.

We carried with us only two rolls of bed sheets with which we had tied some belongings together. These we loaded on the cycles, and we started walking. By now, it was dusk. Unfortunately, we had just sold our horse, and so everyone had to walk. We didn't even have a bullock cart nor were any tongas (horse-drawn carriages) available.

We were shocked when we reached the Kanjrur Dattan area. We witnessed a mass exodus of the entire town. Firing and arson had taken place, and it appeared to be well synchronised and well organized. Everyone was moving towards the Dera Baba Nanak bridge, which was about nine kilometres away. We thought from there we could cross the river Ravi to reach India. Everyone was extremely tired, but we were happy that we would cross over to the other side soon.

As we neared the bridge, about twenty men on horseback came riding at full gallop. They were brandishing swords and muskets and were shouting. They were looting and killing all the Hindus and Sikhs who wanted to cross the bridge. We had no time to think. Most of the motley crowd ran and hid behind the railway line without a fight. My father, with his double-barrel Winchester gun, was the lone man left standing. He immediately loaded his gun and fired at the two horsemen in front.

They were only a few yards away. I was standing just behind him, holding his coat. He had some six or seven cartridges. That was all. But this was a do-or-die situation. He managed to hit the front rider, and so all of them turned around and galloped back towards the bridge. We were told by a survivor of a previous attack that it would not be possible to cross the Ravi river because it was flooded. We left our cycles, loaded with whatever we had, along the railway line embankment and hid in the fields of maize and corn some distance away. Later, we realized that whatever we had brought had been looted by our own men!

My father and an MLA from Veeram Datta, who too had a gun, stood guard but did not know what to do next. It was a harrowing experience. We were lying in muddy corn fields, without any food or water and waiting for death. We had no idea where to go or what to do.

Ultimately, the adults took a strange decision that we would go away from that area, which was infested with dacoits and looters, and find a town or city where there would be police or army. So as the sun set on our second day of leaving home, we found ourselves headed west to Narowal, which was deeper into what had then become West Pakistan. Even today that setting sun is etched in my mind.

By nightfall, we reached a small village with mud huts, and all we wanted was food, water and sleep. There was no food or water, so everyone lay down wherever they were and slept. All that we had been left with were the clothes that we wore, my father's gun and a small attaché case that had his eye operating instruments, the sehra (a headdress worn by the bridegroom) he had worn for his wedding, which was threaded with gold, and my mother's wedding sari. This was saved because the bag was lying under my head when I slept in the corn field. My father's hunting coat that had a few 12-bore cartridges had also been taken because I had put it on my face to ward off the sun.

We were a group of fifteen, my family and our loyal employee Bhai Pal Singh, a Jat Sikh, with his wife and three small children. My youngest sister, Rita, was three years old, and although I was already carrying the attaché case – weighing about fifteen kilograms on my head – I had to also carry her on my shoulder whenever I could to relieve my father. It is a miracle that even Surinder, my youngest brother who was just five years old, walked all this distance on his own without food or any assistance.

When we lay asleep in this village on the second night, my father – and all the adults – were hounded out by a subinspector of police who ordered his subordinate to shoot us. My father flared up, sensing that it was the end and rebuked the subinspector. What kind of a Muslim was he that he was killing unarmed innocents, he asked. The Muslim inspector replied in Punjabi, 'O tun kaun hain chitian kaprian wala menu dasan wala ki thik te ki galat hai?' (Who the hell are you with your white clothes to tell me the difference between right and wrong?) he asked.

My father replied that he was Dr Man Singh, the eye surgeon from Gorala Lallian. The subinspector suddenly fell silent and came up to him and said, 'Doctor Saheb, maino mauf kar deo kionke tusi mare man bap dona da operation kita si' (Please forgive me, Doctor Saheb. You have operated on both my father and mother). My father told him that he would have to let the whole party go, and he agreed.

Then he told my father to go north to Jammu, since Narowal was equally dangerous. The following morning, we changed direction and started moving north without any guidance. More people from the villages had joined us, and it became a long procession moving through an unknown area towards Zafarwal, a big town.

By afternoon on the third day, we reached a Sikh-dominated village, where too everyone was leaving for Jammu. They were better prepared. Many of them had horses and weapons like spears. One set of young Sikh jawans, who were formerly in the army, came to my father and told him that the next village was Muslim dominated, and the people there were attacking, killing and looting anyone on their way to Jammu. This was a big shock to us. But, they said, they would lead our group, and it would be better if my father gave them his double-barrel gun and they would give him their smaller 16-bore single barrel gun.

Since we were a large family, we would be at the rear of the column, and they would return the gun when we reached the border. Everyone was dog-tired, and the children could barely move. My mother was completely exhausted since she had never walked even a few yards in her entire life; she was pleading that she be left to die. We managed to coax her to carry on. My scalp had become so sore from carrying the attaché case with my father's surgical instruments that even touching it was painful. But somehow the instinct to survive egged us on and, by late morning, we too started moving in the direction of the Jammu border. We were a small group of stragglers; the rest of the crowd had left much earlier.

As we neared a village, through which the dirt track passed, a Dogra soldier in civil clothes met my father and told him that we should follow him if we wished to survive and informed us that the morning group had been attacked after crossing the village. There were many casualties. These were the people we would have been with! We had no choice but to follow him.

As we emerged from the village, we saw a big pile of small weapons like spears, axes and takuas (small axe to chop wood) that the group had used to defend themselves. I saw my father's double-barrel gun in that heap and pointed it out to him, but he asked me not to look and carry on. A policeman in uniform was guarding the heap. As we emerged from the village we saw a huge Muslim crowd with swords, spears and other weapons in the distance. They were shouting 'Nara-e-Taqbir, Allah hu Akbar' again and again. It was the most terrifying moment of my life.

My mother almost fainted. She simply couldn't move, so we requested a person with a buffalo to allow us to get her on to the animal's back. This was done with great effort and someone had to hold on to her. I was carrying the attaché case on my head and Rita, my three-year-old sister, on my shoulder. My elder sister was handling the smaller children, and my father, along with the other men, faced the menacing Muslim crowd who were now shouting at the top of their voices and brandishing their swords and other weapons.

My father raised his arm to show that he too had a gun. The single-barrel 16-bore shotgun must have looked like a rifle from their side, so the attacking crowd hesitated. We quickened our step under the directions of the Dogra and walked as fast as we could, our pace increasing in the face of certain death. The gap between us and the attacking crowd was widening.

After about an hour of this traumatic march, when we

didn't know whether we would live or die, we managed to leave the threatening Muslim horde behind. We all slowed down. By late afternoon on the fourth day, we finally crossed the Sialkot–Jammu border and entered Jammu. My mother fainted again, but we managed to revive her. There was a small canal, a distributary of the Ranbir canal, with flowing water. We filled our bellies with the dirty water and were very grateful to be alive.

India was still far away because the entire Shakargarh tehsil was in Pakistan now. This was a British design to ensure that Jammu and Kashmir had no road or rail link, except through Pakistan. We could, thus, only cross the border at Madhopur, which was almost a hundred kilometres away. There was no way we could manage to walk that distance, but once again my father's reputation helped us. He was recognized by the Dogra Sub Divisional Magistrate who was controlling the inflow of 'refugees', the name given to the migrating millions.

He sent us hot parathas and lassi, an offering from the heavens it seemed after days of walking with barely any food or water. The following afternoon, he arranged a small bus for us and some other refugees. All fifteen of us managed to board the bus with great difficulty. The bus dropped us at Brahman ki Bari, near the police station, where we passed the night. The next day, we moved to Satwari in Jammu Tawi. My father left us at the railway platform and went to Palace Road where my grandfather's cousin lived. He was a big contractor. The following day, he came and took all of us to his house, where we stayed for the next three days.

Jammu was connected to the rest of India by both rail and road through Sialkot, which was now in Pakistan. My grand-uncle somehow managed to get us seats in the only dak bus (postal bus). We reached Samba, crossed over the Basantar river – by wading through waist-deep water – and then boarded another postal bus. We reached Kathua by evening. This must have been 31 August or 1 September. We had finally set foot on the soil of new India.

We had lost everything. We did not have a single worldly possession other than the dirty clothes on our back. We were bedraggled and our feet were blistered, but we were relieved that we had survived when so many had not. All our priceless possessions were gone – the medical books; the complete library; handwritten journals stored with exceptional care for centuries by our ancestors; handwritten gutkas (small bound books) with details of medical recipes that our ancestors practised; piles of photographs; cameras; silverware; beddings; utensils; most of the hospital instruments bought with donations from the public, for the public; and our two cows, were all irretrievably gone.

We somehow made our way to Gurdaspur district, where the civil surgeon accommodated us in one of the hospital wards, and my father was asked to join duty at Dera Baba Nanak, where there was an urgent need of surgeons because of the large number of casualties coming in from Pakistan.

The superintendent of police of Gurdaspur, who was a friend of my father's, promised us a house, but that evening – when he was visiting a suburb called Tibri – he was shot dead by his own Muslim guard! We decided to move to

Amritsar, where we had a house near Khalsa College. A lot of our relatives were there too.

Travelling on the GT Road was very difficult because there was heavy concentration of Muslims at Batala, and so we moved to a relative's house in Dhariwal from where my father got in touch with his cousin who was in charge of the army's set-up for evacuation of refugees. He sent an army truck to take us to Amritsar. My father left us in the care of his family members, and he travelled to Dera Baba Nanak to operate on the hundreds of casualties that were piling up from the other side of the new border.

He worked day and night, carrying out surgery with primitive tools. In fact, sometimes he even improvised with some carpenter's tools that he cleaned and boiled for half an hour using boric acid. He saved hundreds of lives. Meanwhile, each of our relatives contributed something to help us set up a home again. Fortunately, my father's savings account was in Amritsar, so we had access to some money to pay for our food and rations.

I will end by telling you what I saw was happening to the Muslim refugee columns that were moving under military escort on the GT Road to Lahore. They were only twenty-four kilometres away from the safety of the border at Wagah. There were groups of up to forty thousand Muslims, going from Amritsar to Lahore. From our house, we could see the GT Road and the railway line running to Lahore. Whenever a kafila (column) of refugees had to pass, sirens blew announcing curfew and anyone found moving outside could be shot by the escort.

My uncle was a real mahatma – he gave atta (flour) and wood to all the households in the area and asked them to make chapattis and fill tubs of water before the curfew was sounded. Then, he would place these on a big table by the side of the GT Road so that refugees fleeing from India to Pakistan would have something to eat and drink. After the column passed, the municipal trucks came and loaded the dead and dying and dumped them in a burial ground. Very few were taken to the hospital.

Actually, I don't think any were taken to the hospital, such was the hatred and savagery that was provoked by religious propaganda. We were seeing two aspects of human beings – one of extreme compassion and the other of total depravity. In those weeks so often trains on both sides were halted, looted and all passengers, especially males, mindlessly massacred.

One such train halted behind our house, in Amarkot, and in spite of the firing by the escort, people shot the occupants from the safety of the nearby houses, even before the army could arrive. When the curfew was over, we found our milkman bringing a young girl on his cycle. In his hand was his bloodied sword. He had just collected her from the train, where everyone she knew had been massacred in front of her eyes. The fear and awe on her face told the whole story. The milkman was a bachelor. He married her, and she became a Sikh.

What else is there to say? You tell me.

10

Running a Country

Narendra Bhagat was in the Indian Administrative Service from the Bihar cadre. He is retired now. He was born in Rohtas district of Bihar in 1943.

I was born on 5 October 1943 in in Sasaram in Bihar. My father's ancestral village was in the old Ranchi district, which is now in Gumla district. He was a magistrate during the British regime and, of course, he continued working as such after independence too. I had two mothers. That is to say, my father had two wives.

My father had a dozen children between his two wives. It was only after I grew up a little and became aware of our large family living under a common roof, that I noticed my mother was addressed as Badi Maa, and the other, Chhoti Maa. But as far as I recollect, amongst us siblings, there was no differentiation, and it didn't matter whether you belonged to Badi Maa or Chhoti Maa. We were a close-knit patriarchal family. My father had a commanding position in the house, and although we were a large team, it was a close team. My father, who was the sole earning member, was focused on taking care of the needs, hopes and aspirations of each member of the family.

Bigamy was not an uncommon practice in those days and was accepted as a personal choice. It was not subject to any critical comments from the society in general. Badi Maa had one daughter and four sons. I was the youngest. Chhoti Maa had five daughters and three sons. There was no conflict amongst us siblings about representing one mother or the other. We were all part of one large family headed by our father.

———————•———————

While not common, bigamy and polygamy were legal in India for all communities. A Hindu man marrying multiple women was a fairly accepted practice, especially among the upper classes. Kings and rulers often had many wives, and so too did rich merchants, zamindars and heads of villages. It was usually an indicator of power and privilege. The Hindu Marriages Act, 1955, made bigamy illegal. Since Muslim men are not covered under the law, polygamy is not prohibited for them.

———————•———————

My father was posted in Motihari, and that was where I spent my early childhood. I was just about four when independence was declared and had started going to primary school. Those were wonderful days. At least where we were, there was no distinction on the basis of religion or caste. Even if there was, it wasn't noticeable to my eyes as a young boy.

I had some wonderful friends who were Muslims, and I had lots of friends who were from other castes. The religious distinction, that is so evident these days, didn't seem to exist then. In fact, a Muslim officer lived next door to us, and he had a couple of children who were our age. We were very close friends; we would participate enthusiastically with them during Eid and they would celebrate Diwali and Holi with us. Things were simpler those days. The culture was better.

I don't have specific memories about the day of Independence, but I remember my parents talking about it as I grew older. The whole country was eagerly looking forward to the day. They were all praises for Gandhi and Nehru and the role the two of them played in bringing freedom to India. My parents were euphoric about the country getting its freedom and talked about it often.

They felt distressed about the violence that was happening across the border, of course, but overall, the mood was positive and everyone felt a sense of accomplishment. They didn't talk too much to us children about the bloodshed, perhaps because they thought it was too disturbing to expose us to things like that.

We saw our father's work from close quarters. His bosses initially were British. In fact, even after independence, some British people were still around. I recollect that my father was transferred from Motihari to Purnea, which was on the eastern border of Bihar, and then from Purnea to Munger. When we were in Munger, our neighbour who lived right across the road was a British gentleman who was an officer working in a gun factory.

Munger is known for its gun and cigarette factories. Both these establishments were still functioning, and while most of the British had left, some hung on at least till 1954–55. My father was also very fond of hunting. These British friends, or rather acquaintances, would join him on these shikars. I too went on a couple of hunts with my father.

My father had a Chevrolet. It must have been a 1940 model. He had bought the car early on. He used it to travel for work, as well as for a lot of his sporting activities. He was quite an enthusiast and an avid tennis player too. We even went for shikar in this car. We usually went to Jamalpur for the hunts, which was a place close to Munger, where the railway factory was located. It was a thick jungle. Other kids would come too, including a couple of the British kids.

I remember on one hunt hearing a loud roar, and then a bear appeared. We children were quite scared. My father was the first to take aim and shoot at it. Usually, after his hunting trips, my father returned with a deer or two. Some staff members from amongst the officers' staff would dress the kill. Then my mothers would cook them. They were both great cooks.

By 1955, most of the British people had left. That also ended the cricket matches we played with their kids. Overall, I'd say that there was no sign of ill feeling that these chaps ruled us for more than a hundred years. We lived in harmony.

Through this time, my father was always too busy with his work and other activities, and he didn't have much time to spend with the children or teach us things. But we always had a tutor, no matter where we were. Three or four of us attended classes at home. Our parents were supportive, and there was a great deal of emphasis on education.

We were asked to focus on our studies, and they would take care of all other issues. Despite the fact that we were a large family, none of us felt neglected. Children have different strengths and mental make-ups, even when they are siblings. A couple of my brothers were very good at sports, like my father was. I was more academically inclined.

Early on, when I was nearly twelve, I was admitted to a newly opened government residential school called Netarhart Public School, which was located a hundred kilometres west of Ranchi. My father asked me to take the competitive entrance exam for it. Every year, they took sixty students, based purely on performance in the exams and regardless of the financial situation of the parents.

Once the kid was admitted, they took care of everything. The school was based on the guru–shishya tradition. Hostels were known as ashrams. The house master was known as Ashram Adhyaksh, and his wife was addressed as Mataji. There were twenty students in an ashram. It was a home away from home and they were like parents to us. There was no distinction among the children about caste, religion or money. All we knew was that we were all Indians, and we were all Biharis.

I have fond memories of this school and the lovely, equitable environment there. As long as I was in that school, I was not ever aware of the inequalities outside. The fee structure was such that the poor didn't pay any fees. My father paid a fee. I think it was seventy-five rupees a month, a substantial sum of money then. My father must have been earning four hundred to five hundred rupees a month at that time. None of my siblings joined the school. I was the only one from my family who went.

For my Intermediate, I came to Ranchi and joined St Xavier's College, where I studied science. Following that, I moved on to do BSc Honours and then a master's in botany from Ranchi University. I won a gold medal, and after that I became a lecturer in the same university in the same department. I was quite clear in my mind that I wanted to take a crack at the UPSC and get into government services.

My father had already passed away by the time, and my elder brother was bearing the burden of looking after the family. I had to help him and do my bit, which was why I grabbed the opportunity when I was offered a teaching position. I worked there for five years, but my goal was always to try for the UPSC.

Don't get me wrong – I found nothing wrong with teaching. I was staying in a colony where a lot of the other teaching staff stayed as well. I began to notice that they were always grumbling about something or the other. It was not a satisfying career for most people. Our conversations were only about the university. It was a limited world.

The civil services are never monotonous and provide a number of challenges. The collector's job is the most well known, but the reality is that you get quite a few interesting assignments in your career. In my first attempt, I got into the IRS. There also I wasn't satisfied and tried again, and finally I got through to the IAS. My father also had a wish that one of his children would get into the civil services, and I was happy that I made it.

I was in the Bihar cadre, and my first posting was in the same place my father was posted earlier, Champaran. I stayed there only for a year, but it was a good way to start my career. Then I moved to Purnea, where too my father had once been posted. In fact, the collector allotted me the same house my father was given, where I had grown up. That was a wonderful experience, and I even reconnected with some of my old friends. I got married while I was teaching in Ranchi University and by the time I got into the IRS and later, IAS, we had had three sons and a daughter.

At the time, bureaucrats, IAS folks in particular, were held in high esteem. We were raised to love and serve the country. We were a new country, freshly independent, and patriotism was deeply embedded in our generation. I thought my temperament, and my attitude and disposition to the job at hand did make a difference to the state. I was always determined to stick to the rule of law and tried to deliver to the best of my ability. No matter what the pressures were, I was intent on staying on the right path.

I feel I emerged a winner in all my assignments, even though there was constant political bullying. When I was the collector of Chhapra, I was under a lot of pressure from Patna to get as many MLAs as possible for the ruling party, which was contesting as many as ten assembly seats. But I stood my ground. In fact, the situation got so difficult that I got calls from the chief minister while the votes were being counted, hinting that I tilt the scale in favour of his candidates.

How does a bureaucrat help win elections? If the collector and SP join hands, it is very easy for them to enable any candidate to win the assembly seat. This was the perception that people in general and politicians particulary in Bihar used to hold till at least the 1980s. It often had direct bearing on large-scale transfers of DMs and SP (Superintendent of Police) before the Election Commission's Model Code of Conduct kicked in. I should add that such perception was not entirely off the mark. Do you want to know how they go about it? Let me illustrate with an example. Constituency-wise, the collector and the SP have all the information at their command. Which means for each constituency they know what the population ratio is, what the inclination of the voters is, whether it is based on caste or some other parameters, etc.

Armed with this knowledge, the collector and SP can back candidate X by quietly forming the polling parties that will be suitable to candidate X. If a constituency has hundred polling stations and, say, fifty per cent of them get polling personnel suitable to candidate X from the list he has provided, that is a big boost. These officials are also government servants, but candidate X knows that they are loyal to him, and they will do what is needed on polling day to help him win. Poll officials have some sway.

The second tack is in the requirement of forces to take care of the election process. In areas where X is strong, the collector and SP can conspire and put a very weak force. This force will close their eyes and will allow any unfair practices to carry on. For candidate Y, on the other hand, the collector and SP will place very strict forces in areas where they are strong, and this force will not allow a single discrepancy to occur. This, however, meant a clear departure in conducting the polls in a fair manner. This was all in the 1980s though, and this is not true now. Nowadays, this is difficult to do because of technological advancements and digitization. Today the Election Commission is far better equipped to quickly communicate instructions and guidelines to the concerned officers as well as monitor, in real time, the goings-on on polling days.

You had asked me whether I felt that my work was contributing to the nation. Let me tell you about an incident. I was posted as commissioner of Patna. Before that, I was cabinet secretary, Government of Bihar, when Lalu Prasad

Yadav and subsequently his wife, Rabri Devi, were in power. Then parliamentary elections were announced. The Election Commission found that both the divisional commissioner and the district magistrate had been blacklisted by the Election Commission for some of their actions in the past. The two, thus, had to be immediately shifted.

As soon as the election was announced, a note was sent that these two had to be moved out, and a panel of names was sought to replace them. I didn't know my name was on the list. One day, I was told I had to join as divisional commissioner of Patna. They were given three names and mine was chosen by the Election Commission. I was moved from the Patna Secretariat to the field office.

The divisional commissioner of Patna was in charge of all the parliamentary constituencies under his jurisdiction, which also included the Patna parliamentary constituency. This constituency had the dubious distinction of its elections being countermanded three times in a row on the immediately preceding occasions.

I took it up as a challenge. Mr T.S. Krishnamurthy was the election commissioner then. While he was on a tour of the state – to take stock of election preparedness – his first stop was the Patna parliamentary constituency. We had a review at the commissioner's office. While welcoming the commissioner, I briefed him about our preparedness. I told him flatly that I was determined to turn around the past history of three countermanded elections.

'There will not even be re-election in many polling booths,' I told him. He was very encouraged to hear that. He gave me a pat on my back during the meeting, and we got on with the job. In those days, the divisional commissioner was given overall power to oversee the constituencies under his jurisdiction. That meant deployment of forces, deployment of manpower, etc. Set instructions were given by the election commissioner on how to organize the manpower, forces for each polling booth, patrolling parties and so on.

All deployment prepared by the DM and SP of Patna had to be approved by the divisional commissioner, and I used my powers. Everything was done by the book. A couple of days before the election, I recall, the DM Patna came to me and said, 'Sir, preparations are already done, and I have a simple request to make.'

'Go ahead,' I said.

'Sir, everything has been lined up. You please instil the fear of God in the officers in charge of various police stations. Just instil the fear of God. The rest will be taken care of,' he said.

I got the point. I said, 'Send a wireless message across and ask them to assemble in a conference hall the next day.' The message was sent to all the police stations and officers, right up to the DIG. We had a meeting in the conference hall close to Gandhi Maidan. In the meeting, I supported my colleagues and asked them to do their duty with sincerity. I also cautioned each of them, saying that it was not our job to be concerned about where we were getting posted after the election.

I told them, 'Your DIG is sitting next to me, and the two of us are not concerned about our future postings. Your attitude should be similar. Do your jobs sincerely. Secondly, the DIG and I will be mobile on the day of polling, right from the word go. And if we find any foul play at any location, I won't hesitate to pass the suspension order right then and there.'

What I am trying to say is that if your intentions are good, and if officers are not constantly worried about getting shunted, you can make things work; you can still deliver results. On the day of the polls, the DIG and I were on the move all day. There was regular feedback, and when we returned the next day, we got the report that only a couple of polling stations had been disturbed. The entire thing passed off peacefully. The Election Commission, in a nationally televised interview, proudly took credit for having conducted the election of Patna parliamentary constituency – of all places – without any major incident. These are the kind of incidents one feels satisfied about.

Getting independence was the first step. Keeping the country running in a fair manner, within the bounds of law, is an equally arduous task. If I had moments of triumph, there were also times when I felt despondent. When I was inspector general of prisons, Bihar jails, I found it very frustrating to work with the minister. He was totally unsupportive and never played by the rules.

Being in the IAS, you are focused on the state. On a

national level, you cannot do much. But we used to interact with batchmates and course mates from other places like West Bengal, Tamil Nadu, etc., and in the 1980s and the 1990s our sense was that, by and large, things were all right, we were doing good work, and the country was progressing. You cannot compare what is happening in the country now to what it was in my time.

The bureaucracy is now, to use a strong word, becoming spineless. They don't have the moral strength to stand up to the political masters and instead simply toe the line. Checks and balances in the system have weakened. Anyone opposed to the ruling dispensation at the centre is taken to task. Digital media, social media, fake news, hate speech and all are also doing a lot of damage. Rule of law has become a casualty.

You might be wondering how I can talk about the rule of law now, having worked in Bihar in the 1980s and 1990s. The point is that as a bureaucrat then you could stand up to what was right. It wasn't just me. Many of my friends also stood by their conviction and refused to allow the law to be flouted. All the government could do was transfer you to an insignificant post. But you had your job, and you would get paid.

Even in the chaos of Bihar there was room for an upright and honest officer to stand up and do the right thing. Those who toed the line enjoyed a privileged position, but those who followed their own convictions were fine too. Today if one does not follow the diktats, he or she gets victimized right away. The price to pay for not following the edict was much smaller then. If I was working in today's scenario, I would have found myself in a piteous situation. I am scared to even think about it.

11

A Verse at a Time

Kumud Pawde was born in 1938. She is a Dalit gender activist, an author and is one of the first Dalit teachers of Sanskrit. She retired as the head of the department of Sanskrit, Vasantrao Naik Government Institute of Arts and Social Sciences. She lives in Nagpur.

I was born on 18 November 1938. I was the eldest in my family, among two sisters and four brothers. My father used to assist advocates in the court, though he was not a lawyer himself, and my mother was a teacher. I grew up in a slum called Anand Nagar, near the Nagpur railway station. It was a Dalit colony, and across the road from the slum was Bhide School, which was run by savarnas (upper castes).

My father was a staunch socialist. He used to be a follower of the communist revolutionary M.N. Roy. He was very well read, although he could not study beyond matriculation. In fact, he was one of the brightest students in his village. Every evening, he used to go to the library and read whatever had arrived. He was my idol.

He also travelled quite a bit, as part of his activism, to places like Lahore, Delhi, Calcutta and Benares. He was in Lahore when Bhagat Singh was hanged, and he would talk to us children about the impact that had had on him. He never cared for the rituals of Hinduism. At the time, the Dalit community was mostly Hindu, and every rural or slum-dweller Dalit used to believe in God because living conditions were so poor. If you didn't have faith, you had nothing. But my father rejected all of that.

We were aware of the struggles against the British. We talked about this at home and in the slum. My father was a very balanced person. He used to tell us, 'Maybe the British are wrong and are shooting at us Indians, but we have to remember that we Dalits are able to breathe because of them. If they weren't here, we would be enslaved by the upper castes, and we would be washing their dirty dishes and forced to go into the dungeon of untouchability.'

I was obviously a big fan of Ambedkar. In the slum, we all were. In fact, my maternal grandfather was the treasurer of an organization that used to fund Dr Ambedkar's movement. It was called the Scheduled Caste Federation, and he was responsible for this movement in Nagpur. My mother's family was relatively well off. My maternal grandfather was a jobber in the mill, which used to be a big post at the time. He used to wear shirts with gold buttons on them and had built a three-storeyed house in the slum. It had intricate carvings on the doors, and some seven or eight rooms.

I was very fond of my grandfather, and it was through him that I learned about Ambedkar and what he was doing around the country. My father too was a great fan of Ambedkar, aligning himself with his atheism and the work he did for the downtrodden.

I went to Bhide School across the road, and I think when Independence Day came along, I was in Class 4. The students were lined up on that day, and we were taken in a procession through the streets of Nagpur to celebrate the event. I remember I had a flag in my hand. I felt a great sense of positivity about independence. We all did. We thought that all the negatives about the country, the poverty, especially, would go away with the British and we would be able to build the country anew.

But, of course, things did not go that way. A few months after independence, Gandhi was killed. There was a great sense of shock and loss at the news. Nobody cooked in the slum that evening. The slum was divided between the Dalit Congressis and the Ambedkarites. There were always Gandhi versus Ambedkar debates in these groups. But there was never any hatred towards Gandhi. And the shock of his death was felt universally, irrespective of where you stood on Gandhi versus Ambedkar.

India may have gained independence, but my life as a young Dalit remained more or less unchanged. In school, I was encountering my own caste challenges. I was not allowed to touch the water utensils. If I got thirsty, I was given some water by the peon or a worker. All the upper-caste girls could touch whatever they wanted. Whenever I touched the water pitcher or the glass, the teacher or the peon used to hit my hands with a stick. I was not the first Dalit girl to go to this school, but I was the first one who wouldn't play by their rules. Others did not dare cross the line. But, because of my father's influence, I was a revolutionary.

I thought if every girl in school could drink from these glasses, why shouldn't I? So, every day, I used to come home with swollen palms. Once, my father saw that I was not able to write properly, that I was holding the pen askew, and he asked me what had happened. That was when he saw my palms and the scars of the daily caning. He took it up with the administration immediately and said this was discrimination, and he would take them to court if they did not put an end to it. Remember, he worked in the court, so he was aware of his rights. That brought me some relief.

Hostility and disgust are familiar to me. I am quite grateful for it, in fact. It was this disgust that pushed me towards Sanskrit. One of my classmates' brother was having his thread ceremony. I was not invited to it, but I found myself outside the house, looking at what was going on. The reverberations of the Sanskrit chants wafted towards me and I was entranced. I took in the whole scene – the fire, the incense, the way their heads moved each time they said 'svaha'. I had never seen anything like that before.

I was probably seven or eight at the time. Then, suddenly,

a lady came out and said, 'Hey! What are you staring at?'
She was dressed in silks and pearls, all kinds of finery. She
offered me a sweet and asked me to leave. I was not a beggar,
and I did not want her sweet. 'Was anyone injured because I
watched them?' I asked her and walked away. 'These Mahars
have really gotten above themselves,' she called after me.
Mahar is my caste.

I knew that day that there was some intimate connection
between me and the Vedic mantras. Later, I asked my father
what language it was in, and he said it was Sanskrit. I asked
him if Sanskrit was difficult and whether we could learn
it. He said, 'Why shouldn't you? We are independent now;
the olden days are gone.' He himself used to chant the
Gayatri Mantra.

Sometimes, I would tell my neighbours that I was going
to study Sanskrit, and they too would wonder why. It wasn't
a language of our forefathers, they would say. Anyway, I was
determined, and in Class 9 I took Sanskrit as an elective.
Ambedkar had not been allowed to study the language, and
I told myself the country was now free, and I must do what
he couldn't.

In school, I had a Sanskrit teacher called Gokhale Guruji.
He was a Brahmin, but he saw some spark in me. He
encouraged me to study the language, and it was because
of him that I ended up studying it all the way till my
postgraduation. The progressive and reformist movements
were in full swing at that time. So, there were teachers
who really believed in their profession, and they never

discriminated about caste. They assessed you by your talent only, but there were others who used to insult me indirectly. For example, they would humiliate other students by saying, 'Look at that Dalit girl. Even she knows better than you.'

———●———

The Progressive Movement and the reformist movements were working towards changing the status quo in society and weeding out discriminatory practices, especially the caste system. Art and activism were their tools. The Brahmo Samaj, Aligarh Movement, Young Bengal Movement, were all major reformist movements of the time. Originally led by Raja Ram Mohan Roy, the reformists fought against idol worship, caste oppression and other practices like Sati, child marriage, etc. The Progressive Writers' Association, a motley bunch of writers who came together to fight social evils, was set up in 1936. The Indian People's Theatre Association was its offshoot. The Progressive Movement was very strongly aligned to the Left and the Communist Party of India.

———●———

In the meantime, the situation at my home had become difficult. My grandfather died and we inherited a lot of debt. Money was hard to come by. There were times when we used to starve or only had puffed rice or gram to eat. My siblings and I were determined that irrespective of our financial condition, hunger, caste or other hurdles, we would study. Quite like Ambedkar, who too had studied in London without being able to afford a bellyful. We were all inspired by him.

After I finished matriculation, everyone suggested that I become a doctor. I had good marks in maths and science, but I was not keen on medicine. I said that I wanted to pursue my interest in Sanskrit. That and English literature were my favourite subjects.

The professors in college discouraged me by saying that Sanskrit was a difficult language, and I wouldn't have any exposure to it at my home. But I stood firm. In college too I faced several humiliations. I had an English professor called Mitra. He asked me to spell a word. I knew the spelling, but I was nervous and mumbled something. Mitra told me, 'My dog barks better than you.'

This only made me more determined. I took the dictionary and decided to learn it by heart. We didn't have electricity. So, each night, I would study by the light of a candle. I would prop my head on my wrist because I did not have a table and learn the dictionary all night. I still have marks on my elbow from all the hours it supported my head and the fat book.

But the next time Mitra asked me to spell something, I stood up and said it confidently. To test me, he asked three or four more words, and I got them all right. In fact, I scored the highest marks in English that year, and my answer paper was put up on the notice board so other students could learn from it. Such victories were few, though. My Sanskrit professors used to routinely insult me. They used to say that I was contaminating the text by reading it. 'You people should not study this.' I never answered back. My only reply was the marks I used to score.

My younger siblings too were facing their own versions of harassment. All of us studied though. We were a large family; some twenty-five of us lived in that three-storeyed home my grandfather had built. We did all the housework and then went to school or college. The pursuit of education was a matter of life and death for us. We were all beaten and pinched in school, but our instinct was to keep quiet about it and work hard.

I finished my BA and then my MA in Sanskrit. I wanted to do a second MA in English. At this time, a young man called Moti Ram Pawde, the son of a landowning Maratha family and a staunch Gandhian, was trying to start a night school for the millworkers. I was not involved in any social work at the time. Moti Ram Pawde's father had some three hundred and fifty acres of farmland, and he was the only son. Yet, his commitment to Gandhi's teachings was so strong that he used to spin his own yarn and make his own clothes.

He was also highly educated. He had five MA degrees, and he was politically active. He had founded an education society. There were lots of mills in Nagpur at the time because cotton was the main crop of central India. People used to discontinue their education in the villages and come and work in these mills. Moti Ram Pawde used to go to the gate of the factories at 3.45 a.m., before the shift began, to convince the labourers to come to his school from 6 to 9 p.m., so that they could continue their education. He didn't have money to pay the teachers, so he persuaded the bright students in the city to come and work as teachers, both as social service and a way to gain some work experience.

Some girl students also wanted to study, and he wanted to get some lady teachers. So, he approached me through my father and said he would like me to be a teacher there. My father was very progressive and said he had no problem, but that I had to agree to it. He knew that I was a 'scholar type' and didn't want to get involved in social programmes. He called out to me and asked me to come downstairs to meet the young man. That day, I was dressed like a typical Maharashtrian woman. I had wrapped a sari and worn a big bindi on my forehead. When Moti Ram Pawde saw me, he fell in love with me.

He asked me if I would come to teach in his school, and I refused. To which he said, 'If you are going to deny education to your own people, why should I bother with them?' Most of the workers were Dalits. This argument appealed to me. I decided to join the school. About twelve hundred students were studying there.

We married in 1962. There was a lot of opposition to it. My husband's father even held a gun to his chest. My family was fine. My father believed in inter-caste marriages. But in the Pawde household there was all kinds of tamasha. Some black magicians were called. They tried to remove the ghost planted by me from his house.

Finally, when his father put the gun on my fiancé's chest, his mother came to his rescue. She told her husband, 'My son has done nothing wrong until now. He has no bad habits. He has been working with Gandhi, who has been talking about the ills of the caste system. If you want to keep the relation, keep it. If you don't want it, even I won't meet him. But do not blame him for choosing whom he wants to marry.' She also pointed out that I was highly educated and right for his son in every way.

It wasn't that my husband's father wasn't educated, but he was feeling pressured by his clansmen. The customs and rituals of the time were such. His friends and relatives used to instigate him saying, 'Had he been our son, we would have killed him.' It was a reaction to that.

By the time I married, I had completed my MA in Sanskrit. I was still pursuing part 1 of MA in English. The financial situation of the family was quite tough. I was desperate for a job, and I was giving interviews in several places. I applied to a whole host of colleges and schools for a teaching position. I was a good student. But in those interviews, I only encountered humiliation.

They used to ask me, 'Do you want to contaminate our children?' 'Has the time now come to learn Sanskrit from people like you?' These were the things I have had to hear. Wherever I saw a vacancy, I applied. For some of these positions, there were no other candidates, but I still wouldn't be given the job. They would laugh at me and say, 'You want us to learn Sanskrit from you?' This despite the fact that my postgraduate teachers used to say that I had perfect pronunciation in Sanskrit. I knew a lot of texts by heart. I used to do well in the interviews, until the issue of my caste came up.

Pandit Nehru was the prime minister then, of course. He would keep talking about merit and opportunities for those who were educated. I wrote a letter to him. I told him, 'You say that jobs are given on merit and that if you are qualified, you will get a job. That is not true.' I also wrote to Jagjivan Ram at that time. Nehru replied to me in a consoling tone. He gave me a scholarship and asked me not to lose faith and keep trying for work.

As long as I was called Somkuwar, I didn't get any job. The minute I married my relatively higher-caste husband – and became Pawde – I got a job. I became a Sanskrit teacher at the government college. There also, initially, there were lots of problems. But because of my interest in Sanskrit and command over the language, the students accepted me. This was the Institute of Social Science and Arts, which is now known as Vasantrao Naik Government Institute of Arts and Social Sciences. I retired as head of the department.

I have four children – three sons and a daughter. They are all quite well educated and have their own careers now.

We should look at whether the lives of the Dalits have improved in independent India through the prisms of social progress, economic progress and dignity. Socially, a lot has changed, but economically, there is much work to be done. A section of society has progressed, but most others haven't.

In the rural sector and slums, people are still struggling. Reservations, they say, have changed the face of the Dalits. Still, ninety-five per cent Dalits are hungry. This is because they are in low-paying jobs. When you see the pyramid of Indian society, the lowest strata are the most hard-working people. And about ninety-nine per cent of the hard-working people are the Dalits and tribals. Today also, the bottom-most rung is occupied by the Dalits.

Reservations benefit only a small part of our population. People in reserved classes who are suffering and hungry do not get the advantage of reservation and are instead defamed for it. The popular perception is that everything goes to the reserved categories. Nothing is farther from the truth.

As for dignity, one has to only read the papers. I have done my post-graduation in Sanskrit. I have been awarded the Sanskrit Pandita. Still, I get humiliated in some church in Kerala where different tumblers are kept for water for Dalits. Or someone is beaten up in Rajasthan because they are Dalit and rode a horse. Or the president of India is not allowed to enter a temple in Odisha. The journey to dignity is very long. The constitution assures dignity and equality. And despite this assurance, we are not getting it. Only the upper class of Dalit society, in academics or administration, get some dignity.

My husband died in 2013. Overall, I have had a successful, happy life. Despite my humiliation, I was happy. I have written books; I have kept myself busy with social and gender activism. I also did a lot of work for the advancement of Sanskrit, for which I got the Sanskrit Pandita Award. Shankar Acharya was the chief guest at the award function. I pinched him on the stage. I told him, 'First, I am a woman, and a woman should not have been learning Sanskrit as per the Manusmriti. Second, I am Dalit, and third, I am married to a Shudra.[1] In all three cases, I should not learn or teach Sanskrit according to your shastras. But the constitution of my India allows me to do this.' He accepted it. He blessed me and asked me to do more work for Sanskrit. That is my vindication.

12

Precision Engineering

S. Vedapuri was born in 1930. He is an engineer who has worked and taught the subject. He also conducts skill upgrading programmes in Coimbatore.

I was born in North Arcot district, near Kanchipuram, in Tamil Nadu. My date of birth is 11 November 1930.

My father was an officer in the revenue department. My mother passed away when I was six months old, leaving behind me, a baby, and my elder sister. My father remarried and my grandparents and stepmother raised me. From my father's second marriage I had four brothers and two more sisters. Eight children. It's a very big family. Most members are now settled near Chennai.

I did my schooling in Cheyyar, near Kanchipuram. In Cheyyar, the freedom movement was run by the local people under the command of loyal leaders. They loved the nation.

They were all arrested. We saw them, my siblings and I, because they were taken by the police to jail right in front of us.

Most of the people were wearing a jubba (kurta) and the Congress cap. They were kept in jail for fifteen days to a month, if I remember correctly, and then they were released. Some of these people lived in our neighbourhood, although I didn't know anyone personally. Since my father was a government servant, he could not be seen indulging in any politics.

These people were bold and dedicated to society. I was intrigued by them but didn't want to participate in these activities myself. I love my country but have always avoided groups and politics and only care about the social welfare of the community. To be honest, I really did not have any idea at the time whether the cause they were fighting for was a worthy one.

There were no discussions in school about what was going on in the country. We just concentrated on what was in the textbook, which we would vomit out for the examination. At home too, people were quite ignorant about what was going on around us. All that my family knew about the world outside was Gandhi and the Congress. At that time, they were the main party. People were also afraid to talk about politics. They were worried about going to jail. My community was a cautious group of people. Our motto was to keep our heads down and mind our own business.

———•———

The freedom movement was as strident in South India as it was in the rest of the country, even though it is less well documented. Certain communities and classes were more active in their participation, while others stayed out of it. Maveeran Alagumuthu Kone, of Thoothukudi district, is considered India's first freedom fighter.[1] He waged a war against the Presidency Armies from 1750 to 1759, some hundred years before the Sepoy Mutiny of 1857. Eventually, he was defeated in battle by the British forces and was executed in 1759.[2]

———•———

After my Class 10, I joined Pachaiyappa's College in Madras for Intermediate and then Presidency College in Triplicane for my bachelor's degree. I was in Pachaiyappa's College on the day of Independence.

The hostel was all lit up. We sang some national songs. I remember we sang Gandhi's favourite bhajans. We were awake for most of the night, but we didn't go out into the city. It was a memorable day. To be honest, we didn't quite understand the meaning of 'swatantra'. It was just a word for us. We were told we would rule ourselves, and we would have freedom. But we didn't know what that actually meant.

We just concentrated on our studies and our future. I was about sixteen years old then, so I didn't have much contact with the real world outside. I hadn't even seen a British person in my life until then. They weren't in the streets or going to offices. They weren't visible to us. They were just a concept.

I finished matriculation, and my uncle suggested that I study BSc Physics so that I could become a high school teacher. That was the level of our ambition. I couldn't score a high rank, so becoming an engineer was not easy. I finished BSc and was almost sent back to the village, where my father was trying to get me a teacher's job.

Surprisingly, we saw an advertisement from PSG Engineering College in Coimbatore. It was only about three lines – a small announcement. My uncle saw it and said it mentioned engineering, and although we hadn't heard the name of the college before, he suggested that I apply. I sent them a postcard. At that time, a postcard was one-twentieth of a rupee, kaal anna. With that, I got a bunch of papers as an application form.

We didn't know how to fill up the form. Somehow, we managed, and I wrote all the details and posted it. After a few weeks I got a reply, asking me to come for an interview. I left Madras for the very first time in June 1951 and reached the interview venue.

They asked me several questions, and I somehow managed to convince them. (*Laughs.*) My family members were surprised to hear I was selected, but I became one of the thirty-eight candidates picked for their Bachelor of Engineering degree. We were all very happy and very proud to become engineers. At the time, Nehru was building the nation. Infrastructure projects and dams were seen as the real assets of the country. So, there was pride in being an engineer.

I did electrical engineering. After that I taught the subject for two years. Then, my godfather, the Principal of PSG College of Technology, sponsored me for training in the UK. I went to Leicestershire first and was there for a year. One day, the welfare officer of the programme came up to me. He had found out that I had completed my BE and BSc. He said, 'Why did you come here? This is not the right place for you.' He suggested I take up a postgraduate course and immediately talked to an officer at the University of Birmingham. I finished my course there.

In Birmingham, there were about thirty of us from all over the world. The duration of the programme was a year and a half, and we didn't have time to think about anything else. I felt like an ambassador from India.

By then I had developed an interest in industrial engineering and management principles. I finished my course and wanted to come back to India. I thought it was my duty to serve my country. We gained everything from this country, and I thought whatever I learned should reach the people in the area where I studied. So, I returned to PSG College of Technology and began to teach there in the early 1960s.

The principal of my college had studied in Durham, UK. He was held up there during the war and his parents thought they had lost him, but somehow he managed to return. He treated me as if I was his own son. In my second year at college, he became an MP and made it his life's mission to provide technical education to the underprivileged. He trained us to help him realize his objectives, and we started conducting education camps for the welfare of the downtrodden. That's how I specialized in human welfare and skill development. I have been doing this for the last sixty or so years.

When I came back to India in the 1960s, financial resources were limited. Management in companies were struggling, and we had to improve the lot of our workers. I focused on that rather than politics. Yes, the country was young, but it was also huge. I was only one person, what could I do? I concentrated on developing my industry and since my institution was attached to educational training, I just applied what I learnt.

I was fortunate to be a professor in an engineering college as well as a works manager in an industrial organization. It was a hectic life. Until 1980, some two hundred engineers were graduating every year from our programme. I was so careless about myself that my health deteriorated. I had to take time off for two years to get my health back. This is something I am always warning young people about. They must take care of their health.

The current state of the country is a debatable point. We have come up in life and we continue to suffer, both at the same time. On the one hand, money is not such a problem now. It is easy to get projects financed. But on the other hand, there is this obsession with working and earning; this mental agony of progress is spoiling the quality of our lives.

It is unfortunate that people are not looking after their health now. Our lives were simpler at the time of independence because of our individual discipline and the feeling that we were here to serve. That is not the case now. Now people have no time to contribute to society, take care of themselves or give time to their families. There are families where parents barely see their kids. They go to office early and come back late, by which time their children are asleep. Often both husband and wife are compelled to work, earn and survive. But at the same time, we have all the comforts.

No one can stop technical and scientific development. Can you imagine it used to take us one week to send a letter to our parents? Now, they are on the other end of the phone. It is heaven now. But people don't know how to handle it.

As a country, we are still climbing our way to the top. Seventy-five years is nothing. It is not easy to build a nation – things take time. We need to be more patient. I think Indian people are clever and sincere. Wherever we go, the Indian brain is greatly respected. We are ahead of several other nations. We should have faith in our own abilities. But whether I am happy with the progress the country has made is a debatable topic. Ups and downs of life are just opportunities for learning.

13

Of Poetry and Prose

Saiyed Anwer Abbas lives in Lucknow. He is an engineer who spent his career teaching at a polytechnic. He is the author of several books on monuments of Lucknow, traditional folk art and Mughal architecture. He was born in 1939.

I was born on 15 August 1939 in Raebareli, Uttar Pradesh. My father was a practising lawyer. He had been a district government counsel since 1924, meaning he could be engaged for government work, although he was not a government employee. My mother was from Iraq. She was the second wife of my father, since his first wife had passed away.

The two families – my mother's and father's – were related. She was sort of like a cousin of his; I am not sure of the exact relationship. What I know is that my grandfathers on the paternal and maternal sides were close relatives. My father's family, it is said, migrated to India at the time of

Shah Jahan's reign. They too came from Iraq and settled in India, where they mostly worked as preachers.

My maternal grandfather had died in Iraq. He had two daughters. My mother was sixteen or seventeen when she got married to my father. She knew only Persian and Arabic. She learned some Urdu and some rudimentary English in India. My father had four children from his first marriage, and five children from the second. So, it was a big family. My mother also died young, in 1949.

I grew up in Raebareli. Then, the three of us siblings – two sisters and myself – were sent to St Francis Convent School in Pratapgarh. In 1946, my father was appointed as a judge in the income tax tribunal. The post was called judicial member. The office was in Allahabad, and the whole family shifted there after my father got the position.

My mother had joined the Communist Party of India. I don't know the circumstances of how and why she joined. She even allowed a party office to be opened in our house. Mr Munshi Kalka Prasad, an old-timer in the party, used to live there. In our house! He lived in the room that served as the party office.

My father was a leader of the Shia community in India. He had been the general secretary of the All India Shia Conference since 1924. My mother also, obviously, belonged to a very religious family; all the men were maulanas. But she was different and not very traditional.

Iraq was also somewhat westernized then, and that had some influence on her too. I have seen her photographs wearing long frocks, which signified a break from the very conservative traditions of the time.

My mother was also an activist for the education of women. Even in our family, women were only educated at home; they were not sent to school. Maulvis came home and taught Arabic to the girls for reading the Quran and Urdu for the purpose of any correspondence they may need to have. Other than that, girls were not taught anything.

But my mother arranged for a more formal education of girls, not just from the family, but also from the neighbourhood. In general, our area and our community were quite orthodox. Women were always in purdah. My mother started wearing the chador, which is basically a big scarf that covers your head, unlike the burqa which covers everything.

She started meeting other family members and asking them to send their daughters to study at the local government school for girls. My elder sisters also went to the school. Then she told the other women to send the girls in a covered tonga, so that the girls would not have to wear the burqa.

In this way, she was a catalyst for ensuring girls' education in our community. She was also engaged in other social work outside the community. A member of the CPI who joined the party later, a lady called Hazira Begum, wrote an article about my mother and that is how I learnt a lot about her early life.

I think my father did have some objection to my mother's activities, especially since he was a senior member of the

Shia Council. But my mother put her foot down. She was stubborn and got her way with him. My mother also organized some protests against the British. I remember walking with her in these processions.

Usually these went around the town, ending at the town hall, which was about two kilometres from our house. Our house in Raebareli, Abbas Manzil, is still standing. The processions would include party workers as well as some labourers. There was some sloganeering, but I don't remember what exactly they were saying. There were probably a couple of speeches at the town hall, and we would return home. The town hall had a clock tower and a large ground. I remember fragments like this. I don't think I understood the implications of British rule at the time.

The school in Pratapgarh was a convent run by Italian nuns. We were the only three inmates of the hostel in the first year. Initially, we had our lunch in the nuns' dormitory. I remember that place very well.

There was a fan that was operated by foot! I was fascinated by the fact that you pushed the pedal with your foot and the fan moved overhead! It was a cloth fan. There was a lot of bamboo in the backyard and a church that we used to visit on Sundays.

In 1946 we moved to Allahabad and were sent to St Anthony's Convent. The school was very close to Anand Bhawan, where Motilal Nehru and later Panditji lived. I remember going there in our car. I think it was

Independence Day, but I am not entirely certain now. There was a function there.

I went with my father. This much I recall. I am not sure if there were any speeches. I guess there must have been some singing. Of course, we were happy that the British were leaving; my mother especially so, since she was active in the movement.

There was no question of moving to Pakistan. My father was elected as the Member of the Legislative Council of UP from a Muslim constituency from 1937 to 1946. He was opposed to the very idea of creating Pakistan. He was a reformist and demanded abolition of separate electorates before independence. He actively disapproved of the partition of India and the formation of Pakistan. Later, he also declined lucrative offers to migrate to Pakistan. In fact, he once actively campaigned for Husain Bhai Lalji of Bombay against Muhammad Ali Jinnah of the Muslim League.

———●———

Excerpt on Jinnah from *Freedom at Midnight*:

A more improbable leader of India's Moslem masses could hardly be imagined. The only thing Moslem about Mohammed Ali Jinnah was his parents' religion. He drank, ate pork, religiously shaved his beard each morning and just as religiously avoided the mosque each Friday. God and the Koran had no place in Jinnah's vision of the world. His political foe, Gandhi, knew more verses of the Moslem holy book than he did. He had been able to achieve the remarkable feat of securing the allegiance of the vast majority of India's Moslems without being able to articulate more than a few sentences in their traditional tongue, Urdu.

Jinnah despised India's masses. He detested the dirt, the heat, the crowds of India. Gandhi travelled India in filthy third-class railway carriages to be with the people. Jinnah rode first-class to avoid them.

Where his rival made a fetish of simplicity, Jinnah revelled in pomp. He delighted in touring India's Moslem cities in princely processions, riding under victory arches on a kind of Rosebowl style float, preceded by silver-harnessed elephants and a band booming out 'God Save the King' because, Jinnah observed, it was the only tune the crowd knew.[1]

Among his Moslems, Jinnah had no friends, only followers. He had associates, not disciples and, with the exception of his sister, ignored his family. He lived alone with his dream of Pakistan. He was almost six feet tall but weighed barely 120 pounds. The skin on his face was stretched so fine that his prominent cheek bones below seemed to emit a translucent glow. He had thick silver-grey hair, and – curiously enough for a man whose sole

companion for 17 years had been a dentist, his sister – a
mouthful of rotten yellow teeth. So stern, so vigorously
composed was Jinnah's appearance he gave off an aura
of steely, spartan strength. It was an illusion. He was a
frail, sick man who already, in the words of his physician,
had been living for three years on 'will-power, whisky
and cigarettes'.[2]

———————●———————

Our family was also connected to the Nehru family. My father's
first wife's brother was the chairman of the Improvement
Trust Allahabad. His name was Haider Mehdi. He was
a Congressman and close to the Nehrus. There are some
references to him in the literature in Teen Murti Bhawan
in Delhi. I was also told that my mother was in Dehradun
to take care of her eldest daughter who was studying there.
At this time, Nehru was interred in the Dehradun jail. She
used to visit him with home-cooked meals on certain days
of the week. She was a very good cook, and he was fond of
her cooking. All these connections tied us firmly to India.

So, there was no discussion at all in my family about going
to Pakistan. We were from here, and we were going to live
here. None of the extended family members were interested
in going to Pakistan, either. All Shias mostly wanted to
stay in India. Our forefathers' graves were here, and we also
wanted to be buried in that earth. My father was offered the

option of being made Pakistan's ambassador to Iran, but he didn't even entertain the idea.

My aunt lived in Lucknow. She was married to the family of the high priest of the Shias, Maulana Kalbe Hussain. Their son, Dr Kalbe Sadiq has been awarded the Padma Bhushan posthumously for social service. Those were the only maternal relatives we had in India. Even in Lucknow, no one we knew went to Pakistan. My father, I think, went to Karachi for a wedding. And that was the only time anyone in our family even visited that country. Much later, one of my stepbrothers married a woman whose family subsequently migrated to Pakistan, and so he did too. This must have been sometime in the 1950s.

I am not sure what conversations others were having with my parents about Partition and moving. We had a very large house, and my father always had an office and a meeting room that was out of bounds for us kids. We were not very close to our father. He was an important person living an important life. We were mostly inside the house with our mother. I remember going to the ladies' club meeting with my mother. But with my father we went out only on Eid or other festivals. Thus, I wasn't privy to the adults' conversations about Partition.

To be honest with you, we didn't hear much about the violence during partition either. Nothing happened in Raebareli or Allahabad. Even Lucknow, which was a bigger town, did not witness any communal violence at the time, if I remember correctly.

After independence, the general mood was one of hope. I remember one poem that I used to recite. The first line of that poem was, 'Naye Hindustan mein hum nayi jannat banayenge' (We shall make a new heaven in new India). In the early days of independence, I was always called upon to recite it whenever people visited our home. That was the sense then – that we had a clean slate to create a beautiful, new country.

Then, when Gandhi died, I remember reading another poem, 'Jagao na Bapu ko neend aa gayi hai' by Shamim Karhani. It was published in an Urdu magazine. I wrote it down, copied it and used to recite it at all functions especially those connected to Gandhi. I did that sometimes even as an adult. Here are a few lines that I remember:

जगाओ न बापू को, नींद आ गई है
अभी उठके आये हैं, बज़्म-ए-दुआ से
वतन के लिये, लौ लगाके ख़ुदा से

(Don't wake up Bapu, he has gone to sleep
He has just come back from an assembly
He has lit the flame from God for the country)

We were very depressed about Gandhi's death. My parents were, of course, great followers and predictably quite upset by the turn of events.

I also remember another incident that had some effect on me. We used to live in the Civil Lines area of Allahabad, which was quite a posh locality. I was very poor in mathematics, so a tutor was engaged for me. He lived in the Old City and used to come and teach me every evening.

When we heard the news on the radio that Gandhi was dead, the tutor immediately started getting anxious. He came to my father and said, 'There will be violence in the streets, and I should go home early.' He was very worried that the killer might be Muslim. We all were. Naturally, there was some disturbance in the city. That did make an impact on me. I was later told the name of the person who killed Gandhi, and we were, perhaps, a little relieved that it wasn't a Muslim name.

I was always quite musically inclined. I could drum very well with my fingers. And later, I taught myself to play the mouth organ. In conservative Muslim families, music was not encouraged. But in my case, no one objected. Even if my father had wanted to, I think my mother would have taken him on. Later, my mother also bought a radio for the home. She also bought me a tabla set for learning music as a hobby in the convent.

After Class 7, I had to move schools again because boys were not allowed beyond that. I finished my Intermediate at Ewing Christian College in Allahabad, where my elder sisters were also studying. One of my sisters did her MSc and joined the university. Then she did her PhD in botany.

The other sister became a doctor at King George's Medical College in Lucknow. She did her MS in gynaecology from

Agra Medical College. They were the first graduate women from our community. Except for my eldest sister, who was married early, everyone else pursued higher education. My eldest sister too graduated, of course, and she worked as an Art teacher in Girls' High School in Allahabad. My father continued with my sisters' education even after my mother died. She had made him promise that he would. And my sisters too were obviously forceful in their desire to continue with their studies.

I pursued engineering. Initially, I worked in various electricity departments – UP, Gujarat State Electricity Board, etc. Then, I came back to Lucknow. I had been selected in the Railway Design and Standards Organisation (RDSO). But my right eye was quite weak. Apparently, I had fallen off a horse as a child and injured my eye.

So, in the RDSO medical test I was told that my vision was a problem, and they would give me another test in three months if I could manage to improve my eyesight. But that wasn't possible. In the meantime, a teaching vacancy at an engineering polytechnic had come up. I joined their electrical engineering department and taught there until I retired in 1997. After my retirement, I started writing. I have written books on Lucknow monuments, architecture and history. My recent book, *Confluence of Cultures*, deals with Hindu, Jain and Buddhist icons in mosques and mausoleums of Gujarat.

I got married in 1966. My wife is my cousin. It was partly a love marriage. My wife's father had died a year before that, and therefore her mother was not agreeing to the marriage. But we told each other we would get married, and so my father went with the proposal. Luckily, everyone agreed, and we were married. Earlier she had passed her Senior Cambridge examination. After marriage, my wife continued her studies and completed her PhD in medieval and modern Indian history from Lucknow University. In 2012, she retired as a professor from a college in Lucknow. We have two children, a daughter and a son. My son, Roshan Abbas, is a media professional and a television personality. My daughter, Shirin, has a PhD in media and journalism.

All the functions of the polytechnic were organized and conducted by me. Be it Independence Day or Republic Day or Gandhi Jayanti, I was the person behind the event. I was very popular with the staff and the students. I used to recite patriotic poems even in college. I was the only Muslim teacher on the engineering side, but there was no othering. I was treated with respect and love by everyone. It was a syncretic culture: there was harmony between the communities. It was a good time.

During this time, we were all quite optimistic about the country. We were proud of all our national achievements. I was going for an interview for my first job when Nehru died. It was a sales job. I learnt that the interview was postponed because of Nehru's death. After that, I did not bother to go back to this company for the interview.

When I was in college, Indira Gandhi had become secretary of the Congress Party. She inaugurated its library building. Since our family was aligned with the Congress – it was either Congress or Communists – this was an exciting event for me.

The Babri Masjid incident was a big event. Except for small riots here and there, until Babri Masjid, there hadn't been any big episodes. In Lucknow, there were more conflicts between Shias and Sunnis than between Hindus and Muslims. After my marriage, I lived in Lucknow, and it was absolutely peaceful. When Babri Masjid happened, we were staying in an annexe in my father's house. It was a mixed population in that area.

My neighbours ran a sweet shop; they were halwais. And they did not belong to a high class. They were middle class; I'd say lower-middle class, even. Some people from the other mohalla provoked them to attack our house. But I heard them telling people that if any harm came to their neighbours, our family, they wouldn't spare them. They warned them off! There was so much harmony.

The other family that stayed across the road was a Jaiswal family, whose girls were studying with my daughter. The kids were friends and went to school and came back together. So, we never felt any animosity. Even after Babri Masjid, we felt safe, although the event itself was shocking.

Now, we stay in a good neighbourhood in Lucknow. It's a nice place to live, there is no ill-feeling between people here. Most people, in fact, keep to their own homes. We greet each other on important festivals. So, I don't feel particularly worried about myself. But when we hear about things that are going on outside our homes today, it does make us a little anxious.

What happens if things get worse, what if more and more Muslims get attacked? Right now, I don't feel fear for myself. But the news of lynching, etc., does affect us. We do find ourselves wondering what the purpose of all this is. Earlier we never thought of ourselves as different. We felt safe as citizens. Sometimes now, if we are in an unknown place or in a crowded unfamiliar place, we feel a bit worried and are cautious, and do not reveal our identity. We have to be careful about what we say, about calling each other by our names. That makes me tense.

I was very optimistic that education and coexistence would lead the country to great success. We would be the leaders of the world. That is what we thought. Now too, it is possible. But communal hatred has increased so much.

Speaking for myself and my family, we have had a very good life. We have managed to live a harmonious life. We have not had to worry about what could happen the next day. I think if we continue living more peacefully, and stop interfering in each other's religious matters, then the country will be fine. That is the meaning of democracy. If India can continue on the path of democracy, it would be very good. We will be one of the finest in the world.

I still feel hopeful about the country. We are better than our neighbouring countries of Pakistan, Sri Lanka, Burma, etc., and even China, as far as democracy is concerned. We can live the lives we want. Everybody loves their own country – the place they are born in, where they studied, where they made their families, where their roots are, their forefathers were. This country is our country.

14

At Close Quarters

Girija Viraraghavan was born in 1939. She lives in Kodaikanal, where she, along with her husband, breeds roses. She is the granddaughter of Sarvepalli Radhakrishnan, who was the second president of India.

My earliest memories are of growing up in Bombay. I was born in 1939. My father was in the railways, what used to be called GIPR – the Great Indian Peninsula Railway. We used to live on Vincent Road in Dadar, which was very close to the railway station. My father would catch a train and go to his office, which was known as Victoria Terminus in those days. I am the older of the two kids, my brother is four years younger than me. Both my maternal grandmother and paternal grandparents were in Madras at that time, and we would spend most of our holidays with them.

My earliest recollections are about playing with my friends in Bombay. We lived in a three-storeyed building with an apartment on each floor. The flat above us belonged to the Patwardhan family. One of the brothers was Achyut Patwardhan, who was very active in the freedom struggle. I was too young to understand, but I remember many comings and goings. I could sense that there was something in the air.

My maternal grandfather, Sarvepalli Radhakrishnan, was a member of the Constituent Assembly from 1946 onwards. He was a professor in Oxford and every time he came to India he would fly in to Bombay. Since we were living there, we would go meet him and spend some time with him, and then he would fly to wherever he had to be in India.

It was a pretty chaotic time to be growing up in. Things were constantly in flux. Just before the independence efforts intensified, we were dealing with the impacts of the Second World War. My father was the rationing officer in charge of the logistics for grains and provisions being carried by the Railways. I remember once that a ship got blown up at the Bombay harbour. The ammunitions in the ship caught fire, along with the bales of cotton in its cargo. There were even gold bars on the ship.

It so happened that my father had gone to see about the rations in some particular warehouse beyond the harbour. When this ship blew up, there was no way he could come back home. For two days there was no sign of him – we had no idea what had happened to him! We were all worried, although my mother tried to stay calm. We only knew that a ship had blown up, and we thought it was the Japanese who had done it. But of course, that was not the case. For three days, the sky was an eerie pink. It was quite something. There were all kinds of stories floating of people finding gold bricks lying on the streets.

———————————•———————————

On 14 April 1944, the British freight ship *SS Fort Stikine* exploded in the Victoria Dock. It was carrying a particularly combustible mix of cargo: cotton bales, ammunition and barrels of oil. It was also carrying thirty-one crates of gold bullion bars! [1]

The cotton and the oil were loaded in Karachi, and the captain of the ship, Alexander James Naismith, recorded his concern about the particularly dangerous mix of the shipment. At around 2 p.m. on 14 April, two days after the ship had docked in Bombay, the crew noticed fire on board. They tried to pump water, but that didn't help matters at all. Nearly two hours later, the crew was asked to abandon the ship, but within minutes, there was a loud explosion, which broke the vessel into two. More than two square kilometres of land was set ablaze; windows broke in homes more than twelve kilometres away. The power of the explosion was recorded by ground vibration as far away as Simla. [2] The exact number of lives lost is unknown – various accounts pitch them between eight hundred and twelve hundred. The captain, Naismith, also died in the explosion.

———————————•———————————

During the war, my father was also an air raid precautions warden. He would go around the neighbourhood in the evening to make sure that all the windows were covered and blacked out. Outside the world of sirens and possible bomb blasts, life was nice for a youngster. I was going to school and playing and growing up with other kids my age. Everything was normal. At least, this was what we thought was normal.

My memories about the freedom movement are all tied around Achyut Patwardhan, or Achyut Mama as we called him. The Indian police was the British police, and they were always looking for him. He was, thus, often evading arrest. Achyut Mama would frequently turn up in different costumes in the building, and we children would wonder why. We thought it was some fancy dress or some such that he was participating in. In fact, we thought he was playing with us. He came as a postman once. Another time, he was a milkman.

On two occasions, he came and hid in our bathroom. I remember asking my parents, 'They have bathrooms in their house. Why is he using ours?' My mother and father said, 'If anyone asks you, don't mention that he is there.' The police did come and knock on our door. Of course, no one told them, and so they couldn't find him.

Once, I remember asking my father why the police were looking for Achyut Mama, and he said, 'That's because he is underground.' Underground? What did that even mean? Shouldn't he be in a cave or something like that if he was underground, I wondered. Instead, he was right there, in the bathroom behind me. It just didn't make sense. We were in that sense a little removed from what was happening in the country.

Achyut Mama often spent time with us. But he didn't talk much about the freedom movement to us children because he was worried about what we would blabber out and to whom. Of course, he would tell us stories, but nothing about the movement or independence. He was very careful. Even in school there were hardly any conversations about the movement.

I went to a convent school, St Philomena's in the nearby suburb of Parel. Mahatma Gandhi's name would be mentioned often. That was pretty much all we knew. And if my grandfather was in Bombay, he would go to see Gandhi. I do remember Gandhi went to Madras once. I was not there, but my cousins went to meet him. They asked for his autograph, and he said that they had to pay ten rupees, which was a huge amount in those days! He said all this money would go to support the movement. Whatever little trinkets and jewellery my cousins had, they donated to the movement. All of this was in the periphery of my life and not at the centre of my existence.

I was excited about Independence Day, but only because everyone around was excited. All the adults were thrilled. On the night of 14 August, my parents and some of their friends crowded around a Philips Radio (if I remember correctly) and listened to Pandit Nehru's 'our tryst with destiny' speech.

They were all so happy – laughing and clapping. Their exhilaration rubbed off on us youngsters. We didn't know the reason, but we knew that something good was happening. It was a happy time.

The celebrations continued on the day after Independence too. Sweets were passed around. We didn't have a car then, but I remember all of us went in a friend's car to central Bombay to see all the public buildings that were lit up. There were fireworks. There was so much happiness everywhere. We were all beaming from ear to ear. I can still see Bombay that day, all decked up, so beautiful. Yet, it didn't really sink in that a big symbolic event had taken place. As far as our lives were concerned, not much changed. My father continued to work in the railways, and we stayed in the same house.

When India became independent, my grandfather represented the country at UNESCO. In 1949, he became the Indian ambassador to the Soviet Union. My father's personal assistant in his office and our cook were taken by him to Moscow, as part of his staff. That was the only thing that really changed in our lives – that we lost some important people of our household. (*Laughs.*)

Before independence, my grandfather was teaching Eastern philosophy at Oxford. He visited us often. For us, he was simply our thaatha (grandfather). When he was made the ambassador, I remember we went and picked him up from the airport, and all the adults were talking about how life would be in the Soviet Union, how cold Moscow was and how he needed to buy winter wear and make sure that

he was properly padded up. He said, 'I am used to Oxford.
It doesn't matter very much. It's nothing I cannot handle.'

We were in Bombay when Gandhi was assassinated.
My father had just come back from office, and when we
heard the news, it was unbelievable. It felt like the world
had stopped. Everything became dark and dim. Everybody
was so affected, it felt like a personal bereavement in each
one's family. I remember feeling the weight of my sadness
that day. Everybody was getting together, trying to get the
latest information, trying to find out what happened. We
were hoping that he had recovered. We didn't know for sure
if he had died in the early hours. We also wondered whether
it was true or the whole thing was just a rumour. Then we
heard Panditji's message on All India Radio. That was when
we knew for sure. It felt like we had lost a member of the
family. We all felt we had known him.

The strange thing was that I don't remember any
conversations at all about the Partition and the dark things
that were happening around the time. It was only a few years
later when we moved to Delhi that we heard the horror
stories. A story that particularly affected me was about two
colleagues, a Hindu woman and a Muslim man, who were
working for All India Radio. They were coming back from
work, and she was so angry at what had happened during the
Partition that she took out a knife and plunged it into him.
In the car, on the way back from work! It was shocking. We
heard lots of stories like that – of anger, of revenge. My father
would come back from work and tell us accounts of people

who had lost everything and how they had to be put up in camps, etc. But in Bombay itself, while it was happening, there was no talk at all about all of this. In the south of the Vindhyas, nobody really knew how bad things had been.

In 1952, my father was transferred to Delhi from Calcutta where we had lived for two years after leaving Bombay at the end of 1949. Then my grandfather came from Moscow, and he stayed with us in an apartment in the newly built MP quarters on North Avenue, which had been temporarily allotted to my father till he was given other official accommodation. Panditji came home, I remember, and he told my grandfather that he would like to propose his name for vice presidentship. This meeting happened in our house. By then, I was slightly more grown up. It was exciting, of course, but we took it in our stride. We didn't really think it was something out of the ordinary. With my grandfather, there were always people dropping in to see him. We were used to it. The vice presidentship only meant that more people would visit our house. It made no difference to us at all.

Nehru came often, and we played cricket with him. He was great fun to be around. When my grandfather was the vice president, my father also managed to get a flat nearby, on what used to be called King Edward Road (now Maulana Azad Road). Every evening, we would go over to my grandfather's home and while the adults exchanged notes on what was happening in the country, the children played cricket in the lawn at the back.

I was always the wicketkeeper. I have a photograph of this with me. As south Indian girls, we wore pavadais (long ankle-length billowy skirts), and it was a great strategy to open your pavadai wide and keep the wicket. No ball would slip past. (*Laughs.*) It wasn't just Nehru. Other prominent people who came to visit my grandfather, including foreign dignitaries, would be invited to play with us. They would troop into the back lawn, and all of us would play together. It was a very informal time. There was no security. It felt like one large family.

I didn't really know much about life before, so I couldn't really make the comparison about whether life had become better after independence or not. It was a period of such complex changes – so many politicians, each vying for their own things, each with their own agenda, it felt that even though we were independent, the country continued to be complicated. At my grandfather's house, they would talk about how things were working out. It was interesting. It was exciting. But it seemed all too complex.

Despite my grandfather's role in the government, my life and the world my parents, brother and I inhabited was completely normal. Was I influenced by my grandfather and seeing Nehru and other important men around him? Not really. But I did often help him tie his trademark turban made of crisp, starched, white muslin cloth, and whenever I accompanied him to various events where he was a speaker, I would carry his notes of points for his extempore talks. As I grew up, I was keen to know more about our history. I realized even then that the history we were taught in school was only of the last hundred to two hundred years, and I wanted to know more about our ancient past. I did my BA in history. That apart, I had no grand thoughts about the country.

I graduated with honours, and then I got married. It was an arranged marriage. My husband had just become a probationer, an IAS officer. He was sent to Mussoorie for training, after which he was posted to the Andhra Pradesh cadre. We lived in Hyderabad and various other parts of the state.

When I was just married and was the wife of an IAS officer, I looked at the country with hope. My husband was part of a team of young people who had great aspirations for this new country. They wanted to serve it; they wanted to administer it and continue the good work that the British had started, as far as civil administration was concerned.

Panditji had launched so many schemes that it inspired one to think that the country was on the right path, and there was a great future. There was a lot of anticipation about the good things to come. We were in charge of ourselves – any mistakes were our responsibility, and there was no one else to blame.

After twenty years of service, my husband decided that his love for roses and plants was greater than his desire to stay in the IAS. So, he took voluntary retirement. He was only forty-one and the first officer to take voluntary retirement and not join some place else. In fact, when she heard about it, Indira Gandhi was shocked. 'What? He left the IAS to grow roses?' she asked.

Since then, we have lived in Kodaikanal, breeding roses. He is well known in his field. I knew nothing about roses or gardening. Ours was a totally academic family. The gardener would bring flowers and make arrangements in the house. We would look at them and admire them, but we wouldn't dirty our fingers. Our noses were always in our books. It was only after I got married that I got interested in gardening. I learnt it from my husband, and now we do everything together.

We have a son and a daughter. Our son had just joined medical college and daughter had finished Class 10 when my husband decided to quit the services. It was really difficult in the early years. Those days an IAS officer's salary was unbelievably little, and by the time one paid for various loans and the provident fund, there was hardly any money left for other household expenses. It was a hand-to-mouth existence. The first few years after he took voluntary retirement were incredibly tough because we had managed to save so little. Eventually, it worked out all right.

My husband works with Indian rose species and he hybridizes them. In the last twenty years, he has registered over a hundred rose varieties, and they are grown all over the world, including Japan, the US, Europe and South Africa. He has named two roses in honour of Bapu – one is called Satyagraha and the other, Ahimsa. In fact, since we are speaking today on Gandhi's death anniversary, I put up pictures of them on my Facebook timeline.

The promise of a free India started very well. But India is such a huge country, and it is so disparate – and with so many people pulling it in various different directions – that it is very difficult to try to have one possible policy for everyone. We are pulled back by various problems that have been there for centuries, such as caste. Can you imagine how religion has become such a huge issue now, when it should be a personal, private thing! But, overall, I think we are getting there. We are slow. We go off course, but I feel we come back on track. For such a huge country, we are still a democracy. We aren't perfect.

Contrary to what you may think, we aren't a very political family even though my grandfather was once the president of this country. Neither was he, in fact.

There is no use depending on the government or politicians. If you want to do something, you do it yourself. A lot of good people in India are doing things to make life easier not just for themselves, but also for those who are less privileged. The spirit of Gandhi lives on.

I think to a great extent the pride we felt when India became independent has remained. We feel very happy about things that our country has accomplished. Certainly, there have been events that are a blot on our story, but every country goes through these things. A hundred years is nothing, considering our five thousand-year-old history. There will be ups and downs. I think as long as people are optimistic and willing to do things for themselves, without depending on the government, things will work out.

My grandfather was very conscious that we had to work together if the country was to progress. He was a charming person and could get along with everyone. He had clear ideals, which were his philosophical ideals of what India should be.

I feel a little sad about the current commentary about Nehru though. The internet and twenty-four-hour news channels are throwing up too many things. Somerset Maugham said when he was in Burma he read the newspapers a year after they were published. By then, the news would have become really old, and it made no difference.

It was better when we were not bombarded by news all the time. Now we have so many people rushing in with their opinions as soon as something happens. It sullies everything. I never thought there would be a day when Nehru would not be lauded in this country. Naturally, in hindsight one can see how things could have been done differently. Things change so quickly. Despite all that, I am optimistic.

15

An Awakening

Singaravelu Venkatachalam was born in 1934. He worked in the Life Insurance Corporation. After he retired, he moved to Washington where his son is employed.

I was born in a place called Thiruvarur in 1934, which was then part of Thanjavur district. My parents lived in various small villages in Coimbatore district. My father was a doctor in government service and was posted in dispensaries in rural areas. There was one doctor for perhaps twenty-five to thirty-five kilometres, and he did everything, whether it was gynaecology, paediatrics or whatever was the problem. This one doctor handled it.

When I was nine, my father decided it was time to focus on my education, and that it would be better for me to live in a bigger place and have access to a stable school, instead of moving around from one place to another. So, I was sent to Thiruvarur to my mother's mother who lived in a large house right next to the temple.

We had a typical childhood of those days. Families were large; we enjoyed ourselves with cousins; there were always people to play with. After I moved to Thiruvarur, I used to go to my parents for vacations. Everyone would come visit at the same time and we used to make the best use of it. We played and went for picnics. It went on like that.

I was the eldest of six children. My sister, who was only a year and a half younger than me, was sent to Madras to live with my aunt and go to school there. I joined her there for my high school. And then I went to a place called Vaniyambadi in Arcot district for my college. My sister stayed in Madras from primary school to postgraduation. I was the only one going from here to there. After graduation, I took up a job in the Life Insurance Corporation, and there also every three years, I would move to a new location. (*Laughs.*)

But I had no complaints. It is always a pleasure to live with one's grandparents. During holidays, when I went home, I was my mother's pet. Nowadays, parents don't want to send their children anywhere. They want them under their roof and they want to control everything. But in those days, the main thing, at least in my family, was about getting a good education.

In fact, there was a point when all six of my parents' children were in six different places. It wasn't easy, but their emphasis on education was paramount. There is some background to this. My paternal grandmother was from the village. She studied till Class 2, if at all. She was married at the age of eleven or twelve, when she was not even a teenager, to her own uncle.

Her husband was a member of the Theosophical Society. Every year in Madras, there was an international seminar of the Theosophical Society. My grandfather used to attend this, and he also used to take his wife along for this week-long jaunt. During the seminar, every evening, there was a public lecture. These were always in English. My grandmother would sit there and not understand a word of what was being spoken. She felt so bad about her lack of comprehension that, in fact, she felt she was not a human being at all.

She decided then that at any cost, even if her husband opposed it, she would see to it that her daughters were educated. Sons were always educated, there was no need to decide that, but for daughters it was different. Unfortunately, her husband died early. She had four children and one in the womb when her husband passed away suddenly. But that didn't stop her from pursuing her dream for her daughters.

She took the children and went to Madras. With the help of some friends, she got a house and sent the kids to school. She was determined to do this. Since my father was raised with these values, education was the highest priority of our family. People have the power to rise to their challenges if they are determined to accomplish something. My grandmother showed me this.

In Thiruvarur, my school was a furlong away from home and I remember we had to leave our footwear outside the class. We did not have a very liberal outlook at that time, hardly any exposure in fact, and so we weren't really encouraged to think about political developments or things like that. We knew the war was on. We knew there were demands that the British must leave the country. But we didn't know any details. The British were just a concept in our heads. I don't think I had ever seen a white person when I was a kid. The only thing we would hear constantly were stories about Gandhiji. He was our great champion. Both at home and in school, the only discussion about the independence movement was about what Gandhi had said or done. He visited various parts of Tamil Nadu and, although I never got a chance to see him, there was always great excitement in knowing that he was somewhere close.

I was thirteen years old when India became independent. When the Second World War ended in 1945, I remember, we all got together – all the children in the neighbourhood – and we made the Union Jack and waved it around. It was all fun and games; we didn't know the seriousness of it.

When Indian independence was declared, we did the same. We made the tricolour and waved it from everywhere. The big temple in Thiruvarur was next to our house. On the night of Independence, there was a big puja at the temple. We, of course, did not have any idea of what freedom meant. All we knew was that instead of being ruled by one set of people, we would be ruled by another. We did not think about the details. I didn't even think my own life would be any different.

But by then, I had started noticing things around me. In the villages especially at the time, agricultural labourers, who were usually Dalits, were looked down upon. They were not treated like humans, but like animals. They could not own land, they could not draw water from the wells, and they could not even walk on several streets. The Dravidian movement had started, and there was talk about emancipation of the downtrodden.

Once I remember when I was twelve or so we went to a village to visit a relative. There was a row of houses on one side of the street, and the other side was agricultural land that was fenced off. The landlords used to stay in these homes overlooking their farms. They would sit in the verandas, keeping an eye on everyone and everything. One day, when we were playing, I saw one labourer walking on the other end of the street. They could not come to where the houses were, of course. He was on the opposite side of the road. He had taken off his towel from his head, tied it on his hip and was walking along.

Suddenly, he turned and looked across the road towards the landlords' houses. One of the landlords was sitting on his balcony, surrounded by his aides. Immediately he said, 'What is that fellow doing? Why is he staring?' That was all. In a flash, his aides took their employer's chappal, caught the guy and beat him up with it. That fellow didn't even open his mouth. They were like, 'Why are you looking? Don't look this way.' The man said nothing. He simply allowed himself to be beaten up.

This incident made a big impact on my mind, and I thought about it for days. It was shocking to me that he had done nothing; he had only looked. For that he was punished so painfully and treated with absolutely no dignity. I remember thinking at the time what was the point of freeing ourselves from the British if this is what our society was about. Thereon, I was attracted strongly to the Dravidian movement because I felt it was the right fight – the fight to treat all human beings as equals. The discrimination between one man and another, purely on the basis of birth, had to be stopped. Slowly, I started realizing that freedom gave us the responsibility to act more vociferously in these matters. It gave us room to fight these injustices. In many ways, it also made the zamindars slightly less powerful.

———————•———————

The Dravidian movement started in 1916 with the formation of the Justice Party.[1] The lead-up to this was a series of non-Brahmin meetings and conferences in the Madras Presidency. There was disproportionate representation of Brahmins in government jobs and other senior positions, and the resentment against this had been building up for decades. The main plank of the party was anti-Brahminism, and its early activities were relegated to petitioning the local administrative bodies for non-Brahmin representation in the government. In 1920, it won the election in the presidency and formed the government.

From then until 1937, it won four out of five elections and was in power for thirteen years. It was the only serious contender to the Indian National Congress in the Madras Presidency. Even though the prospects of the Justice Party were fraying, the Dravidian movement grew in strength under Erode Venkatappa Ramasamy, who was popularly known as Periyar. In 1939, Periyar became the head of the Justice Party, and in 1944, he changed its name to Dravidar Kazhagam. Periyar tirelessly promoted the principles of rationalism, self-respect, women's rights and the eradication of caste. His message was one of empowerment. He felt that caste distinction was created to serve the needs of a few and urged people to first develop self-respect and think rationally. Any rationalist could see that the caste system stifles self-respect, he pointed out.[2] He was also the proponent of the theory that the caste system was a north Indian import, a result of Indo-Aryan influence.

In the early years after independence, we used to crack before-and-after jokes. For example, we would say when the British were ruling us, if you saw a policeman, you would run away. After they left, if you saw a company of police lined up by the side of the street, you would go up to them and say, 'Hey, which VIP is coming today?' (*Laughs.*) That this joke was funny was a reflection of the time.

The other, grimmer, truth is that we understood for the first time about what was going on in other parts of India. We heard about poverty and starvation deaths and famines in other states. Prior to this, we had no idea what was going on in the rest of India. We didn't even know what the 'rest of the country' was. By then, I was nearing the end of my schooling. I thought now we had the freedom to do whatever was needed to be done for the welfare of our own selves.

I finished college and got a small job but, a year later, I managed to get a job at the Life Insurance Corporation (LIC). I was part of the first batch of employees who were recruited after the institution was nationalized. The finance minister at the time had said that nationalization was critical for the development of the country. Basically, LIC itself came into being because there were substantial funds available in the hands of insurance companies. There was interference from industry – lots of big industrialists had their own insurance, their own banking so that the money stayed within their system and did not go out to anybody else.

All that was taken into account, and it was decided that these huge amounts of funds that were available should be used for national development. About two hundred and forty-five companies were nationalized, of which maybe seventy were profitable. So, it was felt that the interest of the policy holders was not served by these people. I was happy that I joined an institution that was going to work for the good of the nation. It gave me a sense of pride.

I have very little experience of working in a private company, but I had seen some of my friends who worked in private firms. Whatever your job was, ultimately it gave you a feeling that you were serving an individual, and you were only following the diktats of the owner. In the public sector, the structure has specific guidelines. I felt that I didn't have to put myself in the position of being a subordinate to a superior and stand up and say 'Good morning, sir'.

I am aware of the bad reputation that public sector companies now have, but there are two important things to consider. One, the scale of things in the public sector is huge. Second, the criticism is only from people who had trouble. In the sense that if your claims process is smooth, no one says anything. It's only those who don't have that experience that speak up. You are not hearing the good stories, and you can't miss hearing a bad story! I think that is what contributes to the perception that public sector companies are inefficient. On the contrary, millions of claims are processed smoothly. It's just that no one talks about it. Of course, there is a small percentage of staff members who don't do their work. They create a bad impression about everybody.

For the last twenty years I have been living in the US on a permanent basis. I would describe life in the US as pleasant, especially when it comes to person-to-person interaction. When you meet someone, you say hello to them whether you know them or not. I like that. The other thing I like is the cleanliness and the sense of hygiene. Other than that, there are many problems there too. The political system there is equally broken.

In India, the image of the country and the behaviour of our people have improved, but sometimes, I feel, we just ape the wrong things. The economic condition of the people is better, compared to the early years post-independence. In the villages, I love seeing children going to school. When we were young, only the elite sent their children to school. But now, everyone is prioritizing their children's education. That is good. That gives me hope. People who work as house help, for example, see their employer's children going to school and the effect that education has on them. And so, they too are putting money aside and prioritizing their children's future. It is an incredible transformation.

1947 to 2022 is not a long time in the life of a country that has never known how to live on its own. We should be happy about some things. But unfortunately, our present-day rulers have become like kings. They don't care. People have to wait for five years to express how they feel about the government. Once you are exposed to the world, you should start questioning the government. Everyone can vote, whether you are educated or not, own a piece of land or not. You can become anything.

Now an ordinary fellow who has a cycle shop or a small grocery store, if he gets power, his first instinct will be to improve himself. He must have been longing to live in a big house or drive a big car. Unfortunately, people don't know when to stop while profiting themselves. They lose the perspective of what they are supposed to do. That is the problem with our leadership. They are in it for themselves.

In the US, as long as you are ready to work, you will be happy. Everything is a question of bargaining. The employer will call you and discuss pay increments; you can make your case, say these are your accomplishments, and this is what you deserve. If you don't demand, you don't get it. Here, whether you work or not, you get some increment. There, there is an incentive to work hard. Here, that is not the case, although I am told things are changing.

Naturally, I am proud of my life here. If someone in the US asks me, I will always say I am proud of the country of my birth. When I come to India, I am very happy to meet everybody. I recharge myself and go back. But what I miss most there is human connections. Here, I feel connected to everybody, even to people I don't really know. That is the greatness of our country – the people. There, I do some gardening, I go for a walk, I spend time with my grandchildren. That's a different happiness. India is my past. The US is my present. They are different, but I find my happiness in both places.

[Singaravelu Venkatachalam passed away shortly after our conversations.]

Notes

Introduction

1. 'Day in Pics: The Times of India August 15, 1947', *The Times of India*, 13 August 2013, https://timesofindia.indiatimes.com/articleshowpics/9552701.cms. Accessed on 24 June 2022.

1. The line on the Ground

1. Benoy Bhusan Ghosh, *Dvijatitattva O Bangali* [Two Nation Theory and Bengalees], 1978, p. 68, https://en.wikipedia.org/wiki/Noakhali_riots#cite_ref-30. Accessed on 7 June 2021.
2. Anthony Read and David Fisher, *The Proudest Day: India's Long Road to Independence*, Jonathan Cape, 1997, p. 295.
3. Frank Jacobs, 'Peacocks at Sunset', *The New York Times*, 3 July 2012, https://opinionator.blogs.nytimes.com/2012/07/03/peacocks-at-sunset/. Accessed on 7 June 2021.
4. Lucy Chester, 'The 1947 Partition: Drawing the Indo-Pakistani Boundary', *American Diplomacy*, February 2002, https://americandiplomacy.web.unc.edu/2002/02/the-1947-partition-drawing-the-indo-pakistani-boundary/. Accessed on 11 June 2021.

2. A Reality Check

1. Smita Gupta, 'Comrade Lakshmi Sahgal (1914–2012): Revolutionary, a True Daughter of India', *Social Scientist,* vol. 40,

no. 9/10, 2012, pp. 85–89, http://www.jstor.org/stable/23338888. Accessed on 13 June 2022.

2. Parvathi Menon, 'Captain Lakshmi Sahgal (1914–2012) – A Life of Struggle', *The Hindu*, 17 November 2021, https://www.thehindu.com/news/national//article60453668.ece. Accessed on 13 June 2022.

3. Rising up in Rouse Avenue

1. 'Day in Pics: The Times of India August 15, 1947', *The Times of India*, 13 August 2013, https://timesofindia.indiatimes.com/articleshowpics/9552701.cms. Accessed on 24 June 2022.
2. Ibid.

4. Through the Looking Glass

1. 'The "Quit India" Speech (8.8.1942)', https://www.mkgandhi.org/about-us.html. Accessed on 24 June 2022.
2. Ibid.

5. Neti, Neti

1. T.R. Sathish Kumar, 'A Throwback to Mysore Chalo', *Deccan Herald*, 14 August 2021, https://www.deccanherald.com/spectrum/spectrum-statescan/a-throwback-to-mysore-chalo-1019703.html. Accessed on 26 May 2022.
2. Molly Murphy, 'Mysore Population Wins Democratic Rule in Newly Independent India, 1947', Global Nonviolent Action Database, 19 September 2015, https://nvdatabase.swarthmore.edu/content/mysore-population-wins-democratic-rule-newly-independent-india-1947. Accessed on 26 May 2022.

6. The Nation Builders

1. Chanchal Kumar Sharma, 'Rise and Demise of Nehruvian Consensus: A Historical Review', Munich Personal RePEcArchive, 16 March 2015, https://mpra.ub.uni-muenchen.de/62863/1/MPRA_paper_61434.pdf. Accessed on 31 May 2022.

7. Hijinks in Hazratganj

1. Shashi Tharoor, *Nehru: The Invention of India*, Penguin Books India, 2003, p. 147.

8. A Coming of Age

1. From the 'On This Day' blog of *The New York Times*. Robert Trumbull, 'Gandhi Is Killed By a Hindu; India Shaken, World Mourns; 15 Die in Rioting in Bombay Three Shots Fired', *The New York Times*, 30 January 1948, https://archive.nytimes.com/ www.nytimes.com/learning/general/onthisday/big/0130.html. Accessed on 1 June 2022.

2. 'Assassination of Mr Gandhi', *The Guardian*, 31 January 1948, https://www.theguardian.com/world/1948/jan/31/india. fromthearchive. Accessed on 1 June 2022.

9. A Long Way Home

1. Sushant Singh, 'Why was August 15 chosen as Independence Day?', *The Indian Express*, 15 August 2016, https://indianexpress. com/article/india/india-news-india/why-was-august-15-chosen-as-independence-day/. Accessed on 13 June 2022.

2. Venkatesh Nayak,'Looking to the Stars: How India's Independence Day Was Decided Upon', The Wire, 23 August 2021, https:// thewire.in/history/india-independence-august-15-date-decision. Accessed on 24 June 2021.

11. Running a Country

1. Marathas are Shudras and a caste higher to Dalits, but they are not quite Brahmins.

12. Precision Engineering

1. 'Role of South Indians in Freedom Struggle Not Highlighted: PC', *Business Standard*, 20 January 2013, https://www.business-standard.com/article/pti-stories/role-of-south-indians-in-

freedom-struggle-not-highlighted-pc-112122300233_1.html. Accessed on 1 June 2022.

2. M.P. Sivagnanam, *History of Freedom Movement in Tamil Nadu* (Vidutalai Poril Tamilakam), Tamil Nadu University, 1988.

13. Of Poetry and Prose

1. Larry Collins and Dominique Lapierre, *Freedom at Midnight*, William Collins, 1975, p. 156.

2. Ibid., p. 158.

14. At Close Quarters

1. 'When the Bombay Docks Rocked', *The Times of India*, 11 April 2004, https://archive.ph/20130103083744/http://articles.timesofindia.indiatimes.com/2004-04-11/mumbai/28331064_1_cargo-vessel-explosive-cargo-victoria-dock. Accessed on 1 June 2022.

2. John Ennis, *The Great Bombay Explosion*, Duell, Sloan and Pearce, 1959, p. 84.

15. An Awakening

1. 'Dravidian Movement', Wikipedia, https://en.wikipedia.org/wiki/Dravidian_movement. Accessed on 27 May 2022.

2. G.P. Gopalakrishnan, *Periyar: Father of the Tamil Race,* Emerald Publishing, 1991, p. 29.

Acknowledgements

Thanks, first of all, to the fifteen people who feature in this book. It was a privilege to be entrusted with these stories and an honour to be able to tell them.

To Thundil George Philip, Rajni George, C.M. Jayaraman (Citizens Voice Coimbatore), M. Venugopal and Soma Basu for their help in finding my subjects.

To Tilottama Roy, Hari Menon, Puneet Malhotra, Priyadarshini Narendra, Vinita Pandya Shah, Saba Naqvi, Anurag Bhagat, Amitabh Pawde and Roshan Abbas for facilitating my interactions with their parents.

To M.K. Jawahar Baapu, who very generously shared his memories about the special relationship between his uncle, N.M.R. Subbaraman, and Mahatma Gandhi.

To Sarbajaya Bhattacharya and Sajni Mukherji for their help with the translation of Tarun Kumar Roy's account.

To my publisher, Chiki Sarkar, for not only coming up with the idea for this book, but also holding my hand through the difficult process of writing it. There were several occasions when I lost my head, but she kept hers.

At Juggernaut, to Arani Sinha and Devangana Ojha for their expertise and patience.

To Joy Bhattacharjya, for everything.

juggernaut

THE APP FOR INDIAN READERS

Fresh, original books tailored for mobile and for India. Starting at ₹10.

juggernaut.in

To download the app scan the QR Code
with a QR scanner app

For our complete catalogue, visit www.juggernaut.in
To submit your book, send a synopsis and two
sample chapters to books@juggernaut.in
For all other queries, write to contact@juggernaut.in